A Book for You from:

Sonoma Regional Collaborative

The Volunteer Center of Sonoma County's
Youth Volunteer Corps,
Retired & Senior Volunteer Program
AmeriCorps & AmeriCorps*VISTA
America's Promise Campaign
Points of Light Literacy Connection
Project SCHOLARS
Cool School

THE PRACTICAL ASTROLOGER

THE PRACTICAL ASTROLOGER

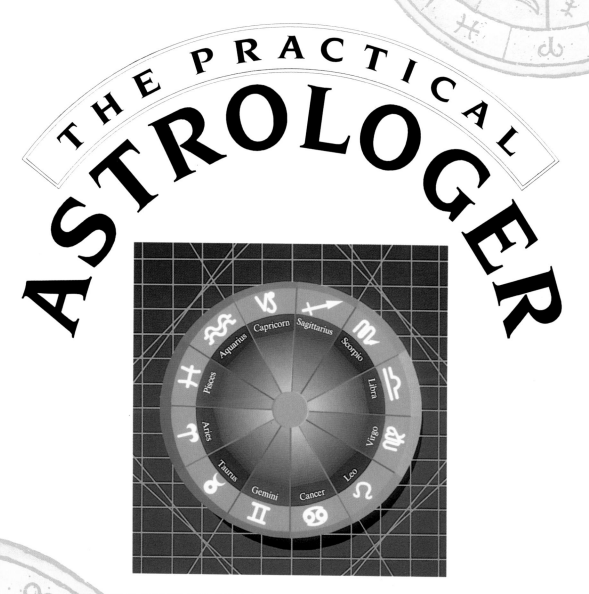

ALL YOU NEED TO KNOW TO CONSTRUCT BIRTH CHARTS,
CAST HOROSCOPES AND DISCOVER WHAT
THE STARS HAVE TO REVEAL

DAVID CHRISTIE-MURRAY

A QUANTUM BOOK

Published by Shooting Star Press, Inc.
230 Fifth Avenue, Suite 1212
New York, NY 10001
USA

ISBN 1-57335-495-3

This book was produced by
Quantum Books Ltd
6 Blundell Street
London N7 9BH

Creative Director: Peter Bridgewater
Art Designer: Ian Hunt
Designer: Sara Nunan
Project Editor: Shaun Barrington
Picture Researcher: Liz Eddison

Typeset in Great Britain by
Central Southern Typesetters, Eastbourne
Manufactured in Hong Kong by
Regent Publishing Services Limited
Printed in Singapore by
Star Standard Industries (Pte) Ltd.

PICTURE CREDITS

All artwork by Lorraine Harrison.
E T Archives pp 2, 10r, 13, 18, 27, 29, 34r, 36r, 41a, 44, 48, 49, 52, 58, 61 centre, 65l, 68,
69, 72, 75, 76, 78, 82b, 85r, 87r, 92r, 98l, 104, 114r, 115r, 119, 121;
TBS Colour Slides pp 3, 9;
C M Dixon pp 9, 10l, 63, 64, 81l, 85b, 89r, 92l, 112r, 113 top left, 115l;
Hutchinson Picture Library pp 19, 106;
Mary Evans Picture Library pp 29, 34l, 35l, 35r, 37, 38, 40, 43, 46, 47a, 50, 54a, 55–57, 65r,
66, 67r, 71 centre, 71r, 73l, 83l, 85 top left, 90l, 94, 97, 98r, 98br, 99, 112l, 113b, 114l, 116,
120, 123;
All-Sport Photographic pp 35 centre, 44;
CBS Records pp 39, 59;
J.S. Library pp 41b, 47b, 74r, 84a, 100 top right, 101a, 102, 103;
Epic Records p 54b;
Ann Ronan Picture Library pp 60, 61, 73r, 74 centre, 81r, 83r, 86l, 89l, 90r, 91, 93, 95, 105,
107, 108, 109, 111, 117, 122;
Adrian Murrel p 61;
Pictorial Press Ltd p 70;
Robin Scagell p 82;
Science Photo Library pp 84b, 87l, 125;
Liz Eddison pp 85, 100l;
Photoresources pp 88, 99r, 113, 118;
Aston Martin p 100br;
Quarto Publishing pp 101b, 103br.

† CONTENTS †

CHAPTER ONE

BASIC DEFINITIONS
CALCULATIONS AND METHOD

This book is entitled *The Practical Astrologer* because it describes, step by step, exactly how to erect a horoscope. Each stage of the procedure and its place in the general scheme is carefully explained as it arises. The student will not turn into an expert straight away, but he will see how easy the basic process is and how great the interest that can be derived from it. However, before we plunge into the practicalities, let us first consider a few general points.

The first step for the would-be astrologer is to discard the idea that astrology is a superstition mingled with magic and the paranormal which can only be understood by mystics steeped in occult lore. Astrology was probably the first systematized science in man's history. Until a few hundred years ago it was synonymous with astronomy, and today it still uses exactly the same tables as do the astronomer and the navigator. Although there have been astrologers down the ages who have professed to have strange powers and who have wrapped their art in mystical trappings – and such individuals can still be met with even today – anyone who simply has the patience to learn can acquire the skill to cast and interpret a horoscope. To be a *first-rate* astrologer on the other hand, considerable sensitivity is certainly needed, for the best interpretations come from more than mere formulaic, mechanical explanations of the meanings of the symbols. Indeed, individuals who are psychically gifted (more than averagely aware of and sensitive to character and atmosphere) may find that a horoscope acts as a kind of focal point for a perception wider and deeper than the face value of the zodiacal and planetary positions.

The beginner's second step is to trust his own ability to make simple calculations. Mathematics is not this author's strong point and if *he* can work out horoscopes there can be very few of his readers who will not be able to match him.

A third step is to adopt the right mental attitude. *Do not expect a horoscope to reveal the subject's inescapable future, and certainly not your own.* The problem of "predestination versus free will" can be left to the theologians; for the purposes of practical living we should agree with Shakespeare when he wrote, "The fault, dear Brutus, lies not in our stars but in ourselves that we are underlings" (*Julius Caesar*). An individual can always be, within the limits imposed by those circumstances of life which cannot be altered, the master of his fate. What astrology does claim to do is to describe *tendencies* in the characters of individuals, to suggest crises and opportunities which may come to them, and to advise how characters such as theirs should react to these circumstances when they do arrive.

PUTTING PEN TO PAPER

The first step in constructing a horoscope is to draw a circle. The larger this is, the more convenient, for although it is not necessary to mark every one of the 360 degrees of its circumference, every 30° around it must be marked, for planets are to be placed accurately which may be at say 13°, 73°, 95° and 117°. The centre of the circle is the place, calculated as accurately as possible for latitude and longitude, at which the event for which the horoscope is being erected occurs. The maker of a chart for a happening in the northern hemisphere pictures himself standing at the centre of the circle looking directly south. This is because the zodiac (the imaginary belt in the sky along which the planets move) occupies a space about 8° on either side of the *ecliptic*. The ecliptic is the apparent path of the sun in the heavens as it follows its annual circle from west to east and it and the zodiacal belt are to the south of the observer. Thus the east will be to the observer's left, the west to the right and the north behind. We are so used to looking at maps with the north at the top of the page and the east and west to the right and left respectively that it takes a little time to adjust to the directions being reversed in this way.

Two more simple steps are to be taken before any calculations are made. A horizontal diameter is drawn across the circle from due east to due west, dividing it into two halves of 180° each. The point where the horizon touches the circum-

WHAT IS A HOROSCOPE?

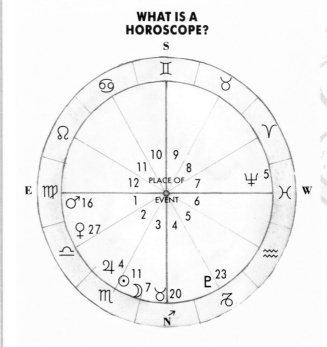

ABOVE The complete chart records the positions of the signs of the zodiac and of the planets and the relation of both to the houses – the symbols, etc. are explained in the following pages.

A horoscope is simply a diagram of the sky, drawn according to certain easily understood conventions, at the hour when, and seen from the place where, an event happens. This is usually a birth, but it can be anything – a marriage, the opening of a new factory or the launching of a ship. On this diagram are marked the positions of the heavenly bodies (Sun, Moon and planets) as they were or will be at the time of the event. (Astronomers know where the Sun, Moon and planets will be at any time in the future, so horoscopes can be drawn for events yet to

happen.) On the diagram are also marked the position of the zodiacal belt (an imaginary belt in the sky along which the principal planets move at different speeds) at the time of the event, and twelve divisions called "houses." These three elements – planets, zodiac and houses – are the skeleton of the horoscope, which is then fleshed out by an interpretation based on the characteristics ascribed to the planets, signs and houses, and the relationships which they have with each other, including the angles ("aspects") formed between the planets.

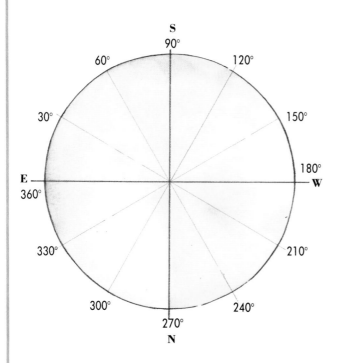

ABOVE The basis of the chart – a circle divided into twelve segments of 30° and marked into 360° beginning at "9 o'clock" (0° and 360°) and measuring the degrees clockwise.

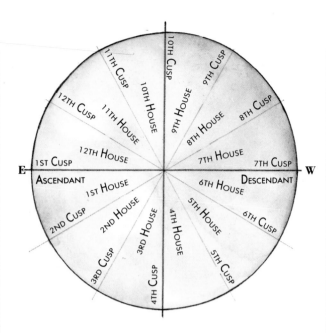

ABOVE The ascendant in the east, the descendant and the position of the cusps of the houses.

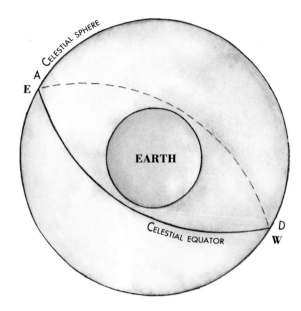

ABOVE The earth is regarded as being at the centre of a hollow celestial sphere on the inner surface of which are set the fixed stars. AD is the ecliptic, the apparent path of the sun through the heavens.

ference to the east is known as the *ascendant*. This is because the anti-clockwise spin of the earth causes heavenly bodies to appear to rise above it. The western horizon is called the *descendant*. For the purposes of astrology, the Earth is regarded as static, with the other heavenly bodies moving relative to it, not it to them.

The next step concerns the twelve divisions of the horoscope known as "houses." These divisions, representing spheres of human activity, were assigned to the planets as their "homes." (Because they are concerned with earthly interests the houses are sometimes called "mundane.") There are many different house systems and this particular division of houses would not necessarily be acceptable to other astrologers. However, this, the equal house system, can be used by the beginner until he knows enough to make his own choice among the various other systems. To divide the circle into houses radii are drawn at 30° intervals, giving twelve segments (or "Tunes"). The segment from the horizon due east then northward (ie from the ascendant downward) is the first house; the next, corresponding to from 8 o'clock to 7 o'clock, is the second; the next, from 7 o'clock to 6 o'clock, the third, and so on. The radii that mark the boundaries of the houses are called "cusps." The cusp of the first house is the radius along the horizon to the ascendant, the cusp of the second is the boundary between the first house and the second, and so on, anti-clockwise, round the circle.

The positions of the houses never change, even though the positions of other elements in the horoscope are in a constant state of flux. The reason for this is that, as already stated, for the purposes of astrology the Earth is regarded as static, with other bodies moving relative to it. As the houses are, as it were, "imprinted" on the Earth as it is at the time of the event, they do not move in relation to it.

Since the Earth turns anti-clockwise, the zodiacal belt – the circle of sky which contains the signs of the zodiac – appears to move from north to south, that is, clockwise, and the signs rise in turn over the eastern horizon. The name "zodiac" (which applies both to the imaginary belt which centres upon the ecliptic *and* the diagram representing this belt) is derived from the ancient Greek words *zodiakos kyklos* which mean "circle of animals" or *ta zodia*, "the little animals." There are twelve of these, each occupying a segment of 30° and each sign is named after a constellation. The signs always occupy the same place in space relative to the Earth as they move round it, but over a long period of time the constellations move relative to our world because of the precession of the equinoxes (see page 122), while continuing to occupy the same places in absolute space. When determining the position of a planet in the horoscope, we may find that a planet in one *sign* of the zodiac may be in the *constellation* that precedes it. (This fact is much used as an argument against the validity of astrology by its opponents.)

The whole circle of the twelve zodiacal signs rises over the eastern horizon once every 24 hours, ie each sign takes two hours to "ascend." This explains the importance of knowing the exact time of the event to be studied. The sign rising above the ascendant at the moment the event occurs is important in the interpretation of the horoscope, and the positions of the planets relative to the other signs are determined by it. The implications of a chart with, say, Aries rising at a birth at 8.00 am on a particular date will be quite different from one with Libra rising at a birth at 8.00 pm on the same day. Of course events may also occur when one sign of the zodiac has almost run its two-hour course and another is on its way. Most astrologers accept that the moment which determines the start of the new individual life is that of cutting the umbilical cord, which can be exactly timed. (There are schools of thought which designate other moments, such as that of conception, or of the emergence of the head, or the whole body.) If the cut is made at a time when Aries has but one minute to run of its two-hour passage there will be a strong influence in the horoscope from the next sign, Taurus.

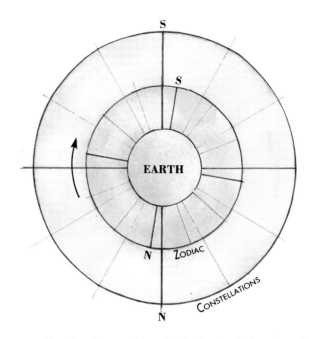

ABOVE The poles and equator of the earth and of the celestial sphere are parallel. The zodiacal belt, moving anti-clockwise, passes through the stationary houses.

EQUIPMENT AND REFERENCES

The equipment needed to construct a horoscope consists of blank paper, a pair of compasses and a protractor, pens and pencils, rough paper for calculations – squared paper is convenient – and books of tables of epheremides. An epheremis shows the positions of a heavenly body at regular intervals of time. The name epheremis comes from the Greek word for "diary," signifying the ephemerality or changing of the places of the Sun, Moon and planets from day to day. The standard work is *Raphael's Ephemerides*, published for every year from 1827. Also required are a *Pluto Ephemeris*, which calculates the position of this planet before 1933, when it was discovered, and a table

of houses – *Raphael's Tables of Houses for Great Britain and Northern Latitudes* is again standard – although it is also possible to use a simplified system of depicting houses so that no tables are needed. Also required are a gazetteer or atlas for finding latitudes and longitudes of places; a list of standard and zone times throughout the world; a table for converting degrees and minutes of longitude and latitude into their equivalent in time; and proportional logarithm tables for finding planets' positions normally found at the back of tables of ephemerides). Bookshops which deal in esoteric literature may also stock blank horoscope charts already marked out in degrees.

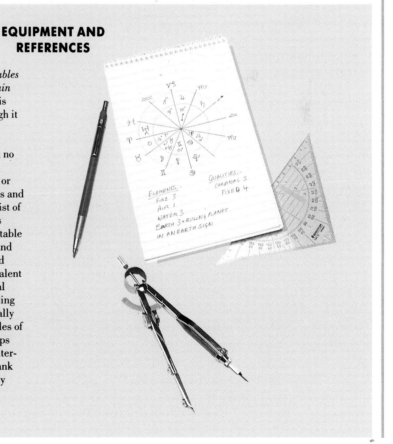

ABOVE Eastern zodiacs included creatures not known in the Western series. This carving of a monkey, an animal from the Japanese zodiac, is an example of the Japanese art of Netsuke, exquisite brooches or fastenings which were originally part of the traditional national costume.

RIGHT A fanciful illustration of the southern sky from Johann Gabriel Doppelmaier's *Atlas Coelestis*, 1742. Parts of the creatures of the zodiac may be seen, together with emblems of other constellations.

THE DATES OF THE ZODIACAL SIGNS

Although we are accustomed to our year beginning on January 1, it was only in the middle of the eighteenth century that it was decided that the year should begin on that date. In the Britain of Bede's day December 25 began the year, and after the Conquest the Normans introduced March 25 as New Year's Day, a date which held sway until 1752. The first sign of the zodiac, Aries, was given approximately the first twelfth of the year, beginning from the spring equinox, March 21. The others were assigned the succeeding twelfths, as shown below. Every sign was attributed characteristics of its own.

The dates assigned to the signs of the zodiac are as follows, although different schools of astrology assign slightly different dates, and astrologers who use the constellations rather than the signs use significantly different dates. The table below gives the dates – and the most usual variations – of each sign, and the dates between which, approximately, the sun appears in each constellation each year. In brackets are the numbers of days in each period. Neither the signs nor the constellations change places at midnight sharp by Greenwich Mean Time on the dates given below, so at the beginning and end of each period there can be a variation of up to a day.

An individual born into the main portions of any of the above periods can say with safety that he is a Gemini or a Leo, etc. But if his nativity took place on one of the borderline dates he will need to know the exact time and latitude/longitude of the event to be certain which is his Sun sign, as it is called. By itself the Sun sign is of little significance. To say, "I'm a Scorpio" is equivalent to saying, "I was born in late October or November," and no more than that. To claim, "I am a Scorpio with Aquarius rising," – that is, in the ascendant at the moment of birth – is to tell the astrologer a little more – but not much.

STAR TIME: THE BASIS OF CONSTRUCTING A HOROSCOPE

Before he can determine which sign is in the ascendant and the relative positions of the other signs, the astrologer has to convert terrestrial time into star, or *sidereal*, time. An explanation of these terms and the method of expressing the one in terms of the other is as follows. (Bear in mind that the 24-hour clock is always used in astrological work. It is easiest to

THE SYMBOLS OF THE ZODIAC

The signs of the zodiac are conventionally known by their Latin names.

ARIES ♈	THE RAM	FIRST
TAURUS ♉	THE BULL	SECOND
GEMINI ♊	THE TWINS	THIRD
CANCER ♋	THE CRAB	FOURTH
LEO ♌	THE LION	FIFTH
VIRGO ♍	THE VIRGIN	SIXTH
LIBRA ♎	THE SCALES	SEVENTH (the only inanimate sign of the twelve)
SCORPIO ♏	THE SCORPION	EIGHTH
SAGITTARIUS ♐	THE ARCHER	NINTH (usually depicted in art as a centaur drawing a bow)
CAPRICORN ♑	THE GOAT	TENTH (often drawn as a goat with a fish's tail)
AQUARIUS ♒	THE WATER CARRIER	ELEVENTH
PISCES ♓	THE FISH (plural)	TWELFTH (portrayed as two fishes embowed, the nose of each towards the other's tail, sometimes connected by a cord with a break in the middle)

The drawings of the symbols first appeared in late mediaeval Greek texts, and their history is unknown. Most of them seem to be a kind of shorthand picture – a hieroglyph – of the sign. The Ram, Bull, Twins, Scales, Archer and Water Carrier (its symbol not unlike the heraldic emblem for water) are all directly suggestive of their emblems. The symbol of the Virgin is reminiscent of a capital M for Mary the mother of Jesus, and the general shape of Cancer's symbol is reminiscent of a crab. There is a sting in the tail of Scorpio's emblem, though its M must not be confused with the M of Virgo. Pisces is represented by two vertical curved lines joined by a horizontal stroke, and the curved lines could just imaginably be likened to fishes standing on their tails.

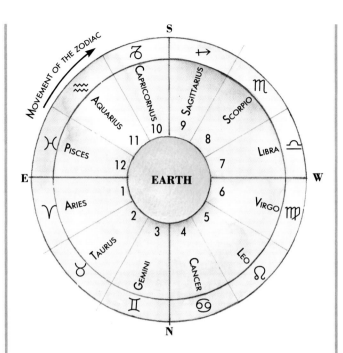

ABOVE The position of the zodiac at the spring equinox, March 21, when the eastern horizon is at 0° Aries. The illustration shows the names and symbols of the signs and the position of the houses.

write hours, minutes and seconds in double figures, thus two hours, six minutes and nine seconds after midnight is 02.06.09; two hours eleven minutes and twelve seconds after midday is 14.11.12.)

The Earth revolves on its axis in 23 hours, 56 minutes, 4.09 seconds, or 3 minutes, 55.01 seconds less than the 24 hours to which our timepieces and pattern of living are adjusted, for obvious practical reasons. The addition of one day in every four years during leap year makes up a fraction more than the sum of the time lost each year, which is compensated for by the fact that the first year of each century, 1800, 1900, 2000, is not a leap year.

Astrology grew up against a background of belief that the Earth was the centre of the universe and, as we have seen, that convention is still observed for the purposes of the measurement of earthly time and the relationship of the planets (including the Sun and Moon) to our world. These were thought to move around the Earth in their orbits within a hollow ball known as the celestial sphere. On the inner surface of this sphere were fixed the stars in their constellations, the positions of which never changed relative to each other. But the celestial sphere *appeared* to move because the Earth was

NAME	DATES OF SIGN	DATES OF CONSTELLATION
1 ARIES	MARCH 21 TO APRIL 20 (31)	MARCH 21 TO APRIL 18 (29)
2 TAURUS	APRIL 21 TO MAY 20, 21 (30, 31)	APRIL 19 TO MAY 10 (22)
3 GEMINI	MAY 21, 22 TO JUNE 21 (32, 30)	MAY 11 TO JUNE 18 (39)
4 CANCER	JUNE 22 TO JULY 22 (31)	JUNE 19 TO JULY 21 (33)
5 LEO	JULY 23 TO AUGUST 22, 23 (31, 32)	JULY 22 TO AUGUST 10 (20)
6 VIRGO	AUGUST 23, 24 TO SEPTEMBER 22, 23 (31)	AUGUST 11 TO SEPTEMBER 17 (38)
7 LIBRA	SEPTEMBER 23, 24 TO OCTOBER 22, 23 (31)	SEPTEMBER 18 TO NOVEMBER 3 (46)
8 SCORPIO	OCTOBER 23, 24 TO NOVEMBER 22 (31, 30)	NOVEMBER 4 TO NOVEMBER 16 (13)
9 SAGITTARIUS	NOVEMBER 23 TO DECEMBER 21, 23 (27)	NOVEMBER 17 TO DECEMBER 13 (31, 29)
10 CAPRICORN	DECEMBER 22, 24 TO JANUARY 20 (28, 30)	DECEMBER 14 TO JANUARY 21 (39)
11 AQUARIUS	JANUARY 21 TO FEBRUARY 19 (30)	JANUARY 22 TO FEBRUARY 14 (24)
12 PISCES	FEBRUARY 20 TO MARCH 20 (29, 30 IN LEAP YEAR)	FEBRUARY 15 TO MARCH 21 (35, 36 IN LEAP YEAR)

ABOVE The *medium coeli* (MC, mid-heaven, zenith) and *imum coeli* (IC, base of heaven, nadir) appear at the south and north poles respectively, for northern hemisphere charts.

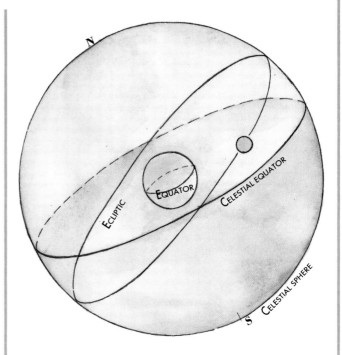

ABOVE The celestial equator, parallel to the earth's equator, crosses the ecliptic (path of the sun) on March 21 and September 21, the two annual equinoxes when the hours of light and darkness are equal.

LEFT Portrait of an astronomer (14th century). He is not actually using a telescope, which was not invented until about 1608, when Galileo used it to prove that the earth moved around the sun.

turning (though this fact was not recognized by the ancients), and as the Earth spins anti-clockwise, the celestial sphere appeared to rotate clockwise.

The Earth's equator, the circle of the globe equidistant from the north and south poles, is paralleled by the *celestial equator*, which is likewise equidistant from the celestial poles. The Earth does not spin upright (if it did the seasons would never change), but at an angle of 23° 27', which means that the Sun's orbit round it does not follow the celestial equator but a path of its own, known as the ecliptic. To an observer on Earth this path passes in front of or through the twelve constellations which make up the zodiac. The two points at which the ecliptic cuts the celestial equator are respectively the spring and autumn equinoxes, March 21 and September 22. Some four thousand years ago, when, arguably, astrology first became a science, the Sun entered the constellation of Aries at the vernal equinox on March 21, so that date was designated 0° Aries and the autumnal equinox therefore became 0° Libra.

The celestial sphere appears to revolve once every time

TABLE 1
SIDEREAL TIME AT DECEMBER 31/JANUARY 1 1890 – 2000 AD

Year	Time	Year	Time	Year	Time	Year	Time
1880	06.40	1910	06.39	1940	06.38	1970	06.41
1881	06.43	1911	06.38	1941	06.41	1971	06.40
1882	06.42	1912	06.37	1942	06.40	1972	06.39
1883	06.41	1913	06.40	1943	06.39	1973	06.42
1884	06.40	1914	06.39	1944	06.38	1974	06.41
1885	06.43	1915	06.38	1945	06.41	1975	06.40
1886	06.42	1916	06.37	1946	06.40	1976	06.39
1887	06.41	1917	06.40	1947	06.39	1977	06.42
1888	06.40	1918	06.39	1948	06.38	1978	06.41
1889	06.43	1919	06.38	1949	06.41	1979	06.40
1890	06.42	1920	06.37	1950	06.40	1980	0641
1891	06.41	1921	06.40	1951	06.39	1981	06.44
1892	06.41	1922	06.39	1952	06.38	1982	06.43
1893	06.44	1923	06.38	1953	06.41	1983	06.42
1894	06.43	1924	06.38	1954	06.40	1984	06.41
1895	06.42	1925	06.41	1955	06.39	1985	06.44
1896	06.41	1926	06.40	1956	06.39	1986	06.43
1897	06.44	1927	06.39	1957	06.42	1987	06.42
1898	06.43	1928	06.38	1958	06.41	1988	06.41
1899	06.42	1929	06.41	1959	06.40	1989	06.44
1900	06.41	1930	06.40	1960	06.39	1990	06.43
1901	06.40	1931	06.39	1961	06.42	1991	06.42
1902	06.39	1932	06.38	1962	06.41	1992	06.41
1903	06.38	1933	06.41	1963	06.40	1993	06.44
1904	06.37	1934	06.40	1964	06.39	1994	06.43
1905	06.40	1935	06.39	1965	06.42	1995	06.41
1906	06.39	1936	06.38	1966	06.41	1996	06.41
1907	06.38	1937	06.41	1967	06.40	1997	06.44
1908	06.37	1938	06.40	1968	06.39	1998	06.43
1909	06.40	1939	06.39	1969	06.42	1999	06.42
						2000	06.41

TABLE 2
ADDITION FOR MONTHS

	Feb		Mar		Apr		May		June		July		Aug		Sept	
	h	m	h	m	h	m	h	m	h	m	h	m	h	m	h	m
Common year	2	02	3	52	05	55	07	53	09	55	11	54	13	56	15	58
Leap year	2	02	3	56	05	59	07	57	09	59	11	58	14	00	16	02

	Oct		Nov		Dec	
	h	m	h	m	h	m
Common year	17	56	19	59	21	57
Leap year	18	00	15	58	22	01

TABLE 3
ADDITION FOR DAYS

Day	Add	Day	Add	Day	Add	Day	Add	Day	Add
2nd	4m	8th	28m	14th	51m	20th	1h 15m	26th	1h 39m
3rd	8m	9th	32m	15th	55m	21st	1h 19m	27th	1h 42m
4th	12m	10th	35m	16th	59m	22nd	1h 23m	28th	1h 46m
5th	16m	11th	39m	17th	1h 03m	23rd	1h 27m	29th	1h 50m
6th	20m	12th	43m	18th	1h 07m	24th	1h 31m	30th	1h 54m
7th	24m	13th	47m	19th	1h 11m	25th	1h 35m	31st	1h 58m

TABLE 4 ADDITION FOR HOURS		
Hours	1–2	Nothing
	3–9	1 m
	10–12	2 m

the Earth rotates, and the timing of the movements of the astrological planets is calculated by their positions against the background of the stars, not by their places relative to Earth (the observer would have to be away from the Earth somewhere in space to see that). The fixed stars are so far distant from the solar system that they do not appear to move at all in relation to it. This means that the time taken for a fixed star to travel from directly overhead at midnight on one night to directly overhead at midnight the next night (which is 360° of the Earth's spin) never varies and is the time accepted by students of the heavens as the standard. It is this star or sidereal time, very slightly different from terrestrial time, that is used in astronomy, astrology and navigation for plotting the positions of the heavenly bodies. The distance between Earth and a fixed star is so immense that the same fixed star will appear to be directly overhead at midnight for millenia of centuries of human observation.

Sidereal time, like solar time, is divided into 24 hours with the same divisions of hours into 60 minutes and minutes into 60 seconds. But the sidereal hour is ten seconds longer than the solar hour, and this has to be borne in mind when converting solar time into sidereal time.

Sets of tables make the calculation of sidereal time simple. We begin with Table 1, which gives the sidereal time at midnight December31/January 1 for the years 1890 to 2000 AD. Table 2 gives the addition in hours and minutes to be made for the month; Table 3 for the day of the month. The first day of the month, being the operative day, is not included. Table 4 gives the addition for each hour.

To show how to calculate sidereal time, let us take as an example a baby whose umbilical cord was cut at 9.00 pm on 29 December, 1958.

Sidereal time for January 1, 1958	06.41
Addition for month (common year)	21.57
Addition for day	01.50
Addition for hour	00.02
TOTAL	29.50

ABOVE Astrology was used in mediaeval times to diagnose illnesses and determine the best time for treatment. Chaucer's "Doctour of Phisick" (for example) "was grounded in astronomye" (= astrology). In this 16th-century engraving, astrologers are casting a birth chart for the child being born to the woman in the foreground.

Since we have to have a time that fits within 24 hours – or, to look at it another way, since 29.51 represents one day plus 5.51 hours – from any total that is more than 24 we subtract 24. The calculated sidereal time of the above birth is thus 5.51. It must be emphasized that the above calculation is merely to show how we arrive at sidereal time – it takes no account of the *place* where the baby was born. The only child of whom this calculation would be true would be one born at 0° of latitude and longitude, where the Greenwich meridian crosses the equator, and the infant would have first to see the light of day on a liner or possibly an aeroplane at a point in the Gulf of Guinea south of Ghana. To arrive at "corrected time," ie time corrected to take into account latitude and longitude, a number of other calculations have to be made.

Since daylight "travels" from east to west, dawn will be earlier in Europe than it is in England and later for an American than for a European. For a birth *east* of the Greenwich meridian four minutes for each degree of longitude east of the Greenwich meridian would need to be *added* to GMT. For a birth in the US four minutes of each degree of longitude *west* of Greenwich would have to be *subtracted*. Allowance for other anomalies such as Daylight Savings Time and, for example, the "mountain time" that is sometimes found in high living localities has also to be made.

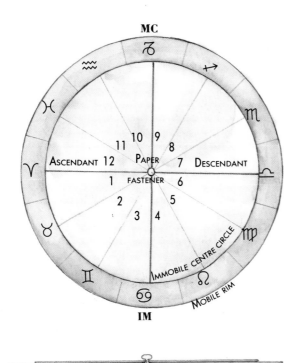

ABOVE A simple tool to make plotting charts easier: the inner circle with the houses marked on it is joined by a paper fastener to another, larger circle, on the rim of which the zodiac is marked.

A USEFUL SHORTCUT

If the astrologer is planning to erect a number of horoscopes, there is a useful piece of apparatus that he can make for himself. From a piece of stiff card cut a circle of a convenient size to act as a basic chart. If it is possible to mark all the 360° on the circumference, so much the better, but at least every five degrees round the whole circle should be marked as accurately as possible. On this draw a horizontal line ending in the ascendant to the east at the left hand and the descendant to the west at the right. If it is intended to use the Equal House system, the circle can be divided by radii into segments of 30° each, numbered for quick reference 1 to 12, the first being that from 9 o'clock to 8 o'clock, the second from 8 o'clock to 7 o'clock, and so on round the circle.

Superimpose the circle on a larger piece of card and mark out a larger circle on this with the same centre as the first. This is cut out in its turn; it will fit round the first like a tyre. round a wheel. The two circles are held together by a paper fastener inserted through their common centre and the larger one moved round the smaller as required.

The larger circle is then also divided into twelve segments of 30° each and the signs of the zodiac are written anti-clockwise on the segments in their order – Aries, Taurus, Gemini, Cancer, Leo, Virgo, Libra, Scorpio, Sagittarius, Capricorns, Aquarius and Pisces. By turning the outer circle clockwise, Aries will rise above the eastern horizon, followed by Taurus and the rest. Thus the student, having discovered what sign is in the ascendant at the time of the event being charted, can move the outer circle to the appropriate position.

He can then cut out ten small pieces of card, each with a pointer protruding from one side, on each of which he draws the symbol of one of the planets. These can be stuck on top of a drawing pin. The pointer is used to indicate the exact degree of the planet's position on the chart – not always easy to point to by the symbols themselves, which are large enough to stretch over several degrees of any circle that can be drawn on an average-sized sheet of paper. With this simple apparatus the astrologer has literally at his fingertips all the elements he needs to plot his charts.

FROM CALCULATION TO INTERPRETATION: THE SIX ELEMENTS

Let us now erect a horoscope for a woman born at Harrow, England, at 1.30 am on July 2, 1951. Following is a résumé of the steps we have to take for the completion of the whole chart and its interpretation.

1. Calculate the sidereal time of birth.

2. From this we find the positions of the signs of the zodiac at the time of birth.

3. From an ephemeris for the year 1951 plot the positions of the planets on the horoscope.

4. To interpret the horoscope we first look at the relationships of the planets to the signs. The zodiacal signs have all been given their own characteristics by astrologers down the ages, as have the planets (see Chapters Two and Three), so a specimen horoscope may have the Sun in Aquarius, the Moon and Mercury in Capricorn, Venus in Pisces, Mars in Sagittarius and Jupiter in Leo, all of which give combinations of characteristics. Taken as a whole, they may complement or contradict each other (which is to be expected, because human beings are a mass of potentials, some of which may be fulfilled at the expense of others. There are contradictions and inconsistencies in the characters of all of us.)

HOW TO CALCULATE SIDEREAL TIME

The calculation of the sign of the zodiac rising at the moment of birth – and the consequent position of the other signs and of the planets – relies upon a geocentric view of the universe. For this reason, adjustments have to be made to the 'terrestrial' time of birth to find the 'sidereal' (or star) time. Though it may look daunting at first, the mathematics is very simple and is standard for all birth charts. Do one, and you can do them all. We have chosen Marilyn Monroe as an example to follow.

Marilyn Monroe was born at 9.09 am, June 1, 1926, local time Los Angeles.

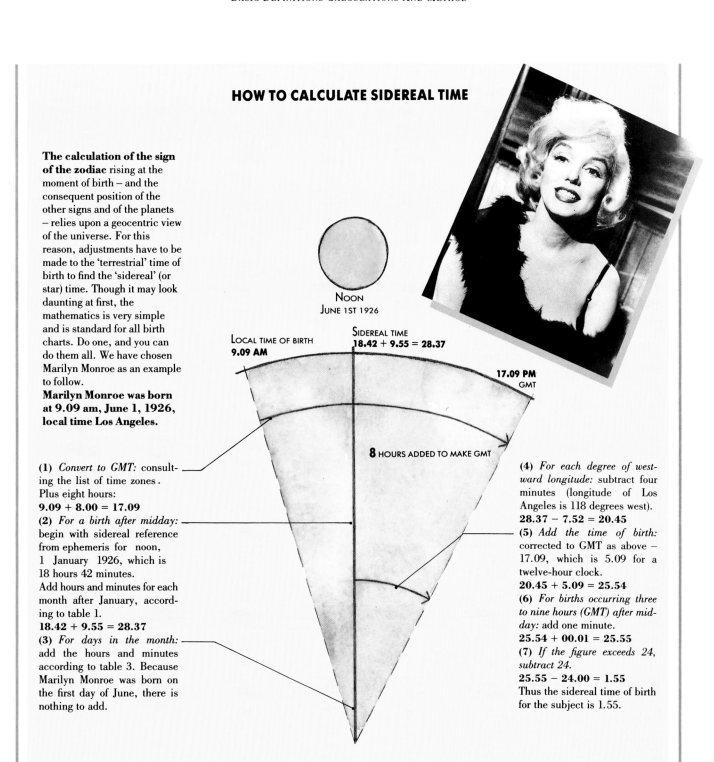

NOON
JUNE 1ST 1926

LOCAL TIME OF BIRTH
9.09 AM

SIDEREAL TIME
18.42 + 9.55 = 28.37

17.09 PM
GMT

8 HOURS ADDED TO MAKE GMT

(1) *Convert to GMT:* consulting the list of time zones. Plus eight hours:
9.09 + 8.00 = 17.09
(2) *For a birth after midday:* begin with sidereal reference from ephemeris for noon, 1 January 1926, which is 18 hours 42 minutes. Add hours and minutes for each month after January, according to table 1.
18.42 + 9.55 = 28.37
(3) *For days in the month:* add the hours and minutes according to table 3. Because Marilyn Monroe was born on the first day of June, there is nothing to add.

(4) *For each degree of westward longitude:* subtract four minutes (longitude of Los Angeles is 118 degrees west).
28.37 − 7.52 = 20.45
(5) *Add the time of birth:* corrected to GMT as above – 17.09, which is 5.09 for a twelve-hour clock.
20.45 + 5.09 = 25.54
(6) *For births occurring three to nine hours (GMT) after midday:* add one minute.
25.54 + 00.01 = 25.55
(7) *If the figure exceeds 24, subtract 24.*
25.55 − 24.00 = 1.55
Thus the sidereal time of birth for the subject is 1.55.

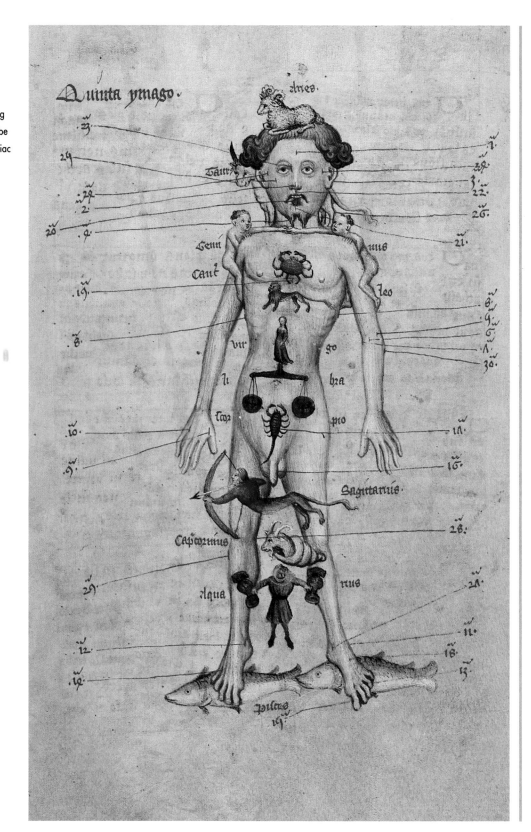

RIGHT "Astrological Man" illustrating the times at which medicines should be taken and also what signs of the zodiac govern which parts of the body.

5. Next we examine the position of the planets relative to the houses (see page 98). The Sun in the fifth house would, for example, give an idea of how the subject of the horoscope would express himself in recreation, the expression of his personal tastes and his love life; the Moon in the fourth house would indicate his relationship with his home and parents; Venus in the sixth house might indicate that he was married to his work.

6. Then comes a study of the aspects of the planets, ie the angles they form with each other in the chart. Some aspects are beneficient, others maleficent, some strengthen the characteristics of the participating planets, others weaken them or cancel them out.

When the astrologer has completed the interpretation of all these, he has all the information he can derive from his chart and can write down his findings in detail. If he is the intuitive type of astrologer, who brings a quality of *psi* or "sixth sense" to his work, he may make a very fair assessment of the character of the subject of the chart. He will probably even have some idea of the kinds of situation such a character might bring about, and how he would and ought to (not necessarily the same thing) react to them.

Let us then begin to plot the chart of our female subject born at Harrow, England. The district has a longitude of less than half a degree west of Greenwich and a latitude of 51 and more than half a degree north of the equator. Note that when we write these completely in figures we should regard them as approximately 51° 40′ N, 0° 25′ W, for there are 60 minutes (60′) in a degree. Avoid the trap of writing half a degree as .5 or 50′, when it should be 30′.

1. CALCULATING THE SIDEREAL TIME OF BIRTH

We have first to establish the Greenwich Mean Time of the birth. In July 1951 British Summer Time (BST) was in operation at Harrow, one hour in advance of GMT. We therefore subtract the hour.

01.30
01.00
00.30

It is possible to buy books of epheremides for every month of every year for periods as long as a century which do away with making additions for the month and day (see bibli-

ABOVE Santosh Perera, a modern astrologer from Sri Lanka.

ography, *The American Ephemeris for the 20th Century, 1900 to 2000 at Noon*). Table 1 gives the sidereal time at midnight on December 31/January 1, 1950/51 as 06.39. To this we add 00.30 for the half-hour after midnight at which the birth took place. 1951 is a common, not a leap year, so we must add, from Table 2, 11 hours, 54 minutes for the month (July), and from Table 3, for the second day of the month, 4 minutes. Table 4 shows that nothing need be added for the half-hour after midnight.

SUMMARY

Sidereal time for December 31/January 1, 1950/51	06.39
Add 0.30 (time of birth)	00.30
Addition for month (July)	11.54
Addition for day (2nd)	00.04
Addition for hours	00.00
	19.07

(Remember that there are 60 minutes to the hour!)

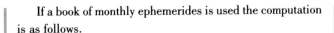
If a book of monthly ephemerides is used the computation is as follows.

Sidereal time for noon, July 1, 1951	06.34.56
Addition for 12½ hours (to bring the time to 00.30 on July 2)	12.30.00
Addition of 10 seconds per hour to convert 12½ hours solar time to 12½ hours sidereal time	00.02.05
	19.07.01

In precision work, for the nearly half-degree that Harrow is west of Greenwich we would subtract two minutes, giving us 19 hours, 05 minutes, but here we are working to the nearest degree of longitude and latitude, which is adequate for most purposes

2. CALCULATING THE POSITIONS OF THE SIGNS OF THE ZODIAC

We have to find first the degree of the sign of the zodiac that lay on the meridian due south on the day and at the time of birth. This southern point is named the *medium coeli* (MC, in translation "middle of the sky" or "mid heaven," also called "the zenith"). Its opposite is named the *imum coeli*, or nadir. For this we turn to Table 5 which gives the MC for each twelve minutes of the sidereal day. 19.07 lies between two times for which zodiacal positions are given:

19.00	14°
19.12	17°

The difference for 12 minutes is 3° or a quarter of a degree per minute. In seven minutes, therefore, passage will have been made through 7 × ¼ degrees = 1¾°, so the degree of the zodiacal sign at the MC will be 15¾ or, to the nearest complete degree, 16°. In marking this on the chart, remember that the zodiac travels clockwise, so 16° of ♑ will be to the right or west of the MC, 14° to the left or east.

The intervals between the degrees of the zodiac are never less than two or more than four per 12 minutes of sidereal time. Table 6 is for quick calculation of these intervals, expressed in fractions of degrees, and the nearest whole degrees to be added for each minute.

The simplest method of fitting in the zodiacal signs, each occupying 30° of the belt, is to mark off a series of 30° segments from either end of Capricorn. This means that Sagittarius occupies the next 30° to the west, Scorpio the next, the descendant will divide Libra 14°/16°, and the

TABLE 5							
Minutes	**Minutes Degree**	**2 Add**	**Minutes Degree**	**3 Add**	**Minutes Degree**	**4 Add**	
1	⅙	0	¼	0	⅓	0	
2	⅓	0	½	1	⅔	1	
3	½	1	¾	1	1	1	
4	⅔	1	1	1	1⅓	1	
5	⅚	1	1¼	1	1⅔	2	
6	1	1	1½	2	2	2	
7	1⅙	1	1¾	2	2⅓	2	
8	1⅓	1	2	2	2⅔	3	
9	1½	2	2¼	2	3	3	
10	1⅔	2	2½	3	3⅓	3	
11	1⅚	2	2¾	3	3⅔	4	

imum coeli and the ascendant divide Cancer and Aries respectively in the same proportions.

This method is used by some practitioners. Others condemn it as over-simplistic and point out that there is an apparent lack of uniformity in the diurnal motion of the Earth (due to the obliquity of the ecliptic), half the signs rising more slowly than the others. In the northern hemisphere these are Cancer, Leo, Virgo, Libra, Scorpio and Sagittarius, and they are classified as signs of "*long ascension*"; Gemini, Taurus, Aries, Pisces, Aquarius and Capricorns rise more quickly and are known as signs of *short ascension*. Leo, for example, can at certain latitudes take more than twice the time as Pisces and Aries to rise completely. In the southern hemisphere the positions are reversed, with the interesting result that more people are born under the Cancer to Sagittarius group of signs in the northern hemisphere and, in the southern, more in the Gemini to Capricorn section.

There are also several methods by which the houses are located. The simplest is the equal house system, which gives each a 30° segment. The cusp of the first house coincides with the radius from the centre of the circle to the ascendant (9 o'clock), the second to 8 o'clock, and so on.

3. PLOTTING THE POSITIONS OF THE PLANETS

We open our ephemeris tables at the page for July, 1951. This gives the positions of the planets on each day of the month at noon sidereal time. (There are tables which give midnight placings, but noon is more generally used.) Since the birth took place at 00.30 GMT on July 2 it is more convenient to take noon on July 1 as our starting point and add whatever alterations need to be made for the movements of the planets, rather than subtract from the noon of July 2.

The first two lines of *The American Ephemeris for the 20th Century* for July 1 and 2, 1951 are as follows:

Day	Sid. time	☉	0 hr ☽	Noon ☽	True ☊	☿	♀
1 Su	6 34 56	8♋50 41	2♊3 42	8♊1 1	12♓7.0	15♋54.2	24♌7.2
2 M	6 38 53	9 47 54	13 57 34	19 53 36	11R 55.6	17 59.1	25 1.5

		♂	♃	♄	♅	♆	♇
		28♊19.0	12♈22.4	26♍28.2	9♋37.8	16♎45.4	18♌15.6
		28 59.7	12 28.5	26 31.5	9 41.5	15 45.5	18 17.1

We first find the position of the Sun at the time of birth. It was at 8 ♋ 50 41 on July 1 and at 9 ♋ 47 54 on July 2. We find how far the Sun travelled from noon on the first to noon on the second day by subtracting the former figure from the latter.

```
09   47   54
08   50   41
     57   13 (57 to the nearest minute)
```

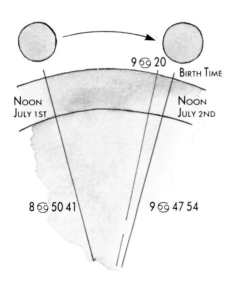

9 ♋ 20
BIRTH TIME

NOON
JULY 1ST

NOON
JULY 2ND

8 ♋ 50 41   9 ♋ 47 54

ABOVE The diagram represents in visual form the mathematical calculation of the sun's position when the Harrow woman was born – noon to noon minus the calculated portion.

We next multiply the Sun's daily motion by the fraction of 24 hours from noon on July 1 to 00.30 + 2′ 5″ (sidereal time) on July 2, ie 12 hours, 32′ 5″. The easiest way to do this is by logarithms. Our subject was born at 12 hours, 32 minutes past noon (we can ignore the seconds). We therefore go to the column headed 12 and run our finger down to 32 minutes. The number is 0.2821 (the 0 is understood). Next, we find 57 in the minute column and in the column headed 0 is the figure 1.4025. We add these two numbers.

```
0.2821
1.4025
1.6846
```

We look for the nearest number to this in the logarithm table. It is 1.6812 which corresponds to 30 in the minutes column (it in fact represents a number a fraction under 30). We can check this by dividing 57 by 2 (= 28½) representing 12 hours' travel and adding 1¾ for the extra half-hour, which gives us 29¾, or a fraction under 30. A pocket calculator gives 29.76 (2′ 45″).

So the Sun's position on July 2 at 00.30 is:

```
08.50.41
00.29.45
09.20.26
```

which may be written 9 ♋ 20.41 and entered on the horoscope at 9 ♋ 21.

The Moon's position at noon on July 1 was 8 ♊ 1.1 and on July 2 was 19 ♊ 53.56. We go through the same process with the Moon and the other planets as we used with the Sun. First subtract its position at noon on July 1 from that on July 2.

```
19   53   36
 8   01   01
11   52   35
               (11 53 to the nearest minute)
```

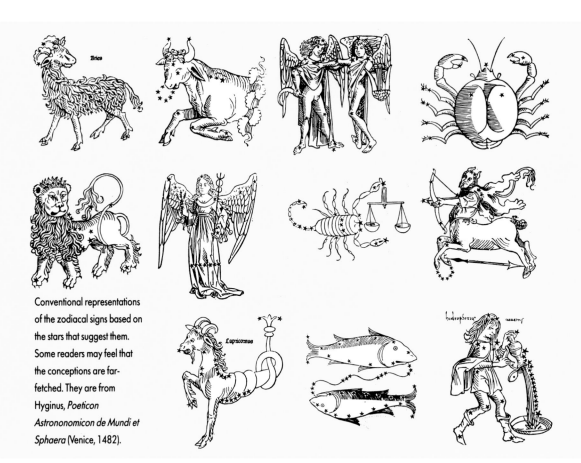

Conventional representations of the zodiacal signs based on the stars that suggest them. Some readers may feel that the conceptions are far-fetched. They are from Hyginus, *Poeticon Astrononomicon de Mundi et Sphaera* (Venice, 1482).

Logarithm of subject's birth	0.2821
Logarithm of Moon's motion	0.3053
	0.5874

The nearest number to this in the log table is 5878, which represents 6′ 12°. Add this to 8   01   01.

8	01	01
6	12	01
14	13	01

The Moon is therefore at 14 ♊ 13 on the natal horoscope. Mercury was at 15 ♋ 54 02 at noon on July 1, 1951, and at 17 ♋ 59 01 at noon on July 2.

17	59	01
15	54	02
2	04	59

Logarithm of subject's birth	0.2821
Logarithm of Mercury's daily motion	1.0614
	1.3435

Nearest number to 1.3435 in log table is 1.5.

15	64	02
1	05	00
16	59	02

Mercury is at 16 ♋ 59 02 in the horoscope.

Venus

At noon on July 2	25	01	05
At noon on July 1	24	07	02
		54	03

The addition pro rata works out at 28, so we have Venus at 54.03 plus 28′ = 54.31, ie 54 ♊ 31.

The results of the above calculations together with those for the remaining planets may be summarized in table form thus:

Planet	☉	☽	☿	♀	♂	♃	♄	♅	♆	♇
Daily motion	00 57.13	11 52.35	02 4.59	00.54.3	00.40.7	00.06.1	00 03.03	00 03.57	00 00.1	00 01.55
Log of birth time difference	0.2821	0.2821	0.2821	0.2821	0.2821	0.2821	0.2821	0.2821	0.2821	0.2821
Log of daily motion	1.4025	0.3053	1.0614	1.4260	1.5563	2.3802	2.6812	2.5563	—	2.8573
Sum of logs	1.6846	0.5874	1.3435	1.7081	1.8384	2.6623	2.9633	2.8384	—	3.1394
Position at 00.30, July 2	08♋51.41	08♊1	15♋54	24♌7	28♊19	12♈22	26♍28	9♋37	16♎45	18♌15
Anti-log correction	0.30	6.12	0.53	0.28	0.21	0.03	0.2	0.2	—	00.00.01
Correct location	09♋21	14♊13	16♋47	24♌35	28♊40	12♈25	26♍30	9♋39	16♎45	18♌15

The positions of the planets can now be entered on the chart. It is wise to write them in such a way that they can be read without having to turn the horoscope round. There is no need now for their positioning on the chart to be exact for interpretation to be made. Provided they are placed in the right houses and the interpreter bears in mind as he works their exact relative positions to the signs, each other, and important points such as the ascendant and mid-heaven, they can be placed as is convenient.

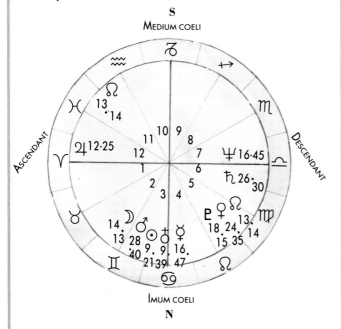

The chart of the woman born at Harrow, England at 1.30am on July 2, 1951.

(See page 26 and Chapter Four.)

4. THE RELATIONSHIPS OF THE PLANETS TO THE SIGNS

This aspect of interpretation is covered by reading the characteristics of the signs and the planets, discussed in Chapter Three, and by applying the principles described in Interpretation, Chapter Four.

5. THE PLANETS IN RELATION TO THE HOUSES

Again, bear in mind the characteristics of the planets, the areas controlled by the houses (see page 98), and apply the techniques described in Interpretation, Chapter Four.

6. ASPECTS OF THE PLANETS

The influences of the planets are modified in a positive or negative way by their angular relationships to each other. These relationships are known as "aspects" and are measured between two planets, or a planet and the ascendant, or MC, or descendant, along the ecliptic in degrees and minutes of celestial longitude.

Astrologers make an allowance, called an orb, of so many degrees, varying from 2° to 8° (see Table 7 below) on either side of an aspect, and regard planets "within orb" as being aspected. These relationships accentuate the qualities associated with the planets, producing strong or weak psychological tendencies which the subject must either use to the good or of which he must be wary.

There are ten aspects, of which five are regarded as important, three as minor and two comparatively insignificant. Astrologers, not surprisingly, vary in their estimation of the values of the lesser aspects.

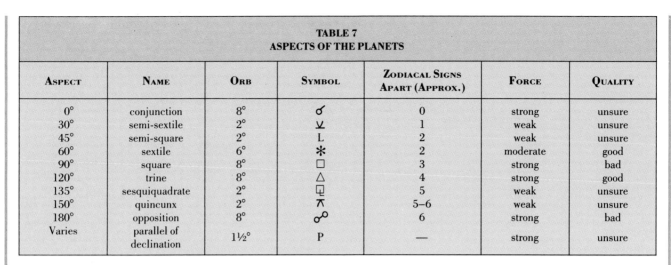

ASPECT	NAME	ORB	SYMBOL	ZODIACAL SIGNS APART (APPROX.)	FORCE	QUALITY
0°	conjunction	8°	☌	0	strong	unsure
30°	semi-sextile	2°	⩗	1	weak	unsure
45°	semi-square	2°	L	2	weak	unsure
60°	sextile	6°	✳	2	moderate	good
90°	square	8°	□	3	strong	bad
120°	trine	8°	△	4	strong	good
135°	sesquiquadrate	2°	⊡	5	weak	unsure
150°	quincunx	2°	⊼	5–6	weak	unsure
180°	opposition	8°	☍	6	strong	bad
Varies	parallel of declination	1½°	P	—	strong	unsure

TABLE 7 — ASPECTS OF THE PLANETS

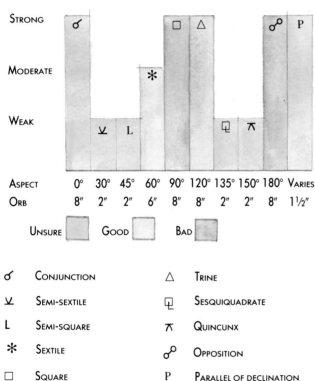

ABOVE The "bar chart" above shows the modification of the effect of the planets by their inter-relationship: reinforcing or weakening each other in a positive or negative way.

The formula for expressing aspects is to write the symbol for one planet, then the glyph for the aspect expressed and finally the second planet's symbol. Mercury in conjunction with Venus, for example, is written

Conjunction: The characteristics of planets in conjunction powerfully reinforce each other.

Semi-sextile: Of minor importance, but indicates conditions requiring a conscious effort by the subject to use or overcome.

Semi-square: See Semi-sextile.

Sextile: Indicates a moderate, harmonious influence of the good characteristics of the planets if equal attention is paid to them and the signs in which they are found.

Square: A discordant force which can cause frustration, imbalance and inner conflict. If the subject has a strong enough personality to use the energies released by the combination of influences, which would overwhelm a weak character, he may be able to turn the situation to his advantage.

Trine: Brings a harmonious influence, more powerful than that of the sextile. A weak character may be harmed by the too-easy success or prosperity that it produces.

Sesquiquadrate: See Semi-sextile.

Quincunx: See Semi-sextile.

Opposition: Indicates tension, even hostility, between the planets and signs involved, possibly resulting in a schizophrenic inner conflict of different sides of personality. The subject who is made aware of this situation can concentrate on developing those characteristics of the signs and planets

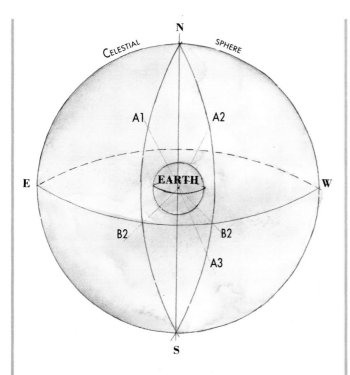

ABOVE Planets A1 and A2 are at the same angle north of the equator and reinforce each other, as do B1 and B2 south of the equator, but are in opposition to A3.

that complement each other, thus removing the clashing elements and evolving a wholeness of personality in which all components find a place and produce a balanced ego.

Parallel of declination: Declination may be defined as the angular distance of a heavenly body from the celestial equator, measured on the great circle passing through the celestial north and south poles and, where measurement is made from Earth, the north-south axis passing through the Earth. Since the celestial and terrestrial equators are parallel to each other, the declination of a planet corresponds with terrestrial latitude and is measured in degrees and minutes north and south of the equator.

Planets with the same declinations are "parallel," reinforcing each other's influences and characteristics if they are on the same side of the equator, but in opposition if on opposite sides. The declination of all the planets except the Moon can be calculated proportionately.

One item remains to be entered on the chart. Every lunar month the Moon completes a nodical revolution of approximately 27 days, crossing the ecliptic twice. One crossing is

from south to north, known as the ascending or north node and represented by the symbol ☊. The other, from north to south, is named the descending or south node, and its symbol is ☋. They are sometimes called respectively the dragon's head and the dragon's tail.

The north node's relationship to sign, house and planetary aspects is thought to indicate benefits received without effort by the native (for example, unexpected largesse from some source such as a legacy). The south node's position, always exactly opposite the north's, indicates handicaps, sacrifices or ill-health in a part of the body associated with the sign in which the node is found. The north node is shown in some epheremides, in others as a "true node," which is not the one to be used. *The American Ephemeris for the 20th Century*, for example, under "Astro-Data" at the bottom of the page gives a "mean" for each month, that for July 1, 1951 being 13 ♊ 12.1. The addition for the second, given on the inside of the front cover, is 3.2 minutes, or 3 minutes 12 seconds, or 192 seconds, or 4 seconds for each half-hour. From 12 noon on July 1 to 00.30 on July 2 is 25 half-hours (plus 2 minutes, 5 seconds for conversion into sidereal time, but this number is insignificant in this instance and may be ignored), so we have to add 100 seconds to 13 ♊ 12.1, giving a total of 13 ♊ 14 to the nearest minute. We may mark in the south node, therefore, at 13 ♍ 14.

7. ADJUSTMENTS FOR RETROGRADE PLANETS

In most horoscopes some planets will be found to be marked R or ℞ which stands for "retrograde." This is because they appear to be moving backwards in their tracks. All the astrological planets except the Sun and Moon are sometimes retrograde: Mercury 20 to 24 days every 3½ months, Venus for 5 to 7 weeks about every 19 months, Mars for 10 to 12 weeks about every 26 months, Jupiter for 4 months at irregular intervals, and Saturn, Uranus, Neptune and Pluto for, respectively, 4 to 8 months, 5 to 7 months, about 5 months, and 5 to 8 months every year. Retrogression is an illusion brought about by the differing speeds and sizes of the orbits of the planets, and is similar to the illusion given to a passenger in an express train that a local train which it is passing is going backwards. If a position for a retrograde planet is to be calculated *before* the given ephemeris time, the interpolation must be *added* because the ephemeris position is less than earlier positions. If a position *after* the ephemeris time is to be obtained, the interpolation must be *subtracted*. Consider the following examples.

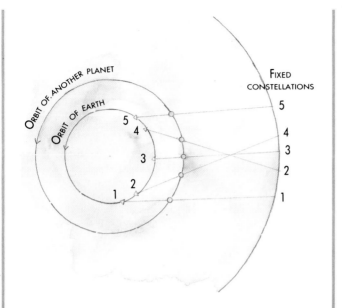

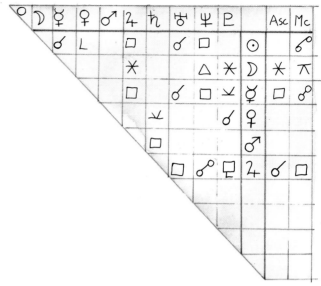

ABOVE Retrograde motion of the planets. The numbers 1 to 5 on the earth represent positions of an observer on successive days of a planet seen against fixed stars. The planet appears to move forwards from 1 to 2, backwards from 2 to 4, then onward to 5.

ABOVE RIGHT A table of the aspects of the planets on the Harrow subject's chart. Read down from the planetary symbol in the top line along to the symbol in the unheaded column; for example, Mercury is in conjunction with the sun, which is in opposition to the MC.

TABLE 6							
S T	**M C**	**S T**	**M C**	**S T**	**M C**	**S T**	**M C**
00.00	0 ♈	06.00	0 ♋	12.00	0 ♎	18.00	0 ♑
00.12	3	06.12	3	12.12	3	18.12	3
00.24	7	06.24	6	12.24	7	18.24	6
00.36	10	06.36	8	12.36	10	18.36	8
0.48	13	06.48	11	12.48	13	18.48	11
01.00	16	07.00	14	13.00	16	19.00	14
01.12	20	07.12	17	13.12	20	19.12	17
01.24	23	07.24	19	13.24	23	19.24	19
01.36	26	07.36	22	13.36	26	19.36	22
01.48	29	07.48	25	13.48	29	19.48	25
02.00	2 ♉	08.00	28	14.00	2 ♏	20.00	28
02.12	5	08.12	1 ♌	14.12	5	20.12	1 ♒
02.24	8	08.24	4	14.24	8	20.24	4
02.36	11	08.36	7	14.36	11	20.36	7
02.48	14	08.48	10	14.48	14	20.48	10
03.00	17	09.00	13	15.00	17	21.00	13
03.12	20	09.12	16	15.12	20	21.12	16
03.24	23	09.24	19	15.24	23	21.24	19
03.36	26	09.36	22	15.36	26	21.36	22
03.48	29	09.48	25	15.48	29	21.48	25
04.00	2 ♊	10.00	28	16.00	2 ♐	22.00	28
04.12	5	10.12	1 ♍	16.12	5	22.12	1 ♓
04.24	8	10.24	4	16.24	8	22.24	4
04.36	11	10.36	7	16.36	11	22.36	7
04.48	13	10.48	11	16.48	13	22.48	11
05.00	16	11.00	14	17.00	16	23.00	14
05.12	19	11.12	17	17.12	19	23.12	17
05.24	22	11.24	20	17.24	22	23.24	20
05.36	25	11.36	23	17.36	25	23.36	23
05.48	27	11.48	27	17.48	27	23.48	27
						(24.00 = 00.00)	

LEFT Portents in the sky in past ages caused consternation. Here the populace show wonder and fear at an eclipse of the sun and astrologers calculate its significance.

1. Find the position of Mars at 6.00 am GMT on March 5, 1965. 6.00 am GMT on March 5 is 6 hours plus 10 seconds per hour sidereal time before noon on that day = 6 hours, 1 minute

Noon position of Mars, retrograde, on March 4, 1965

        20   41.2

Noon position of Mars, retrograde, on March 5, 1965

        20   18.2

Difference for 24 hours   23.0

Difference for 6 hours 1 minute (by calculator, calculation by logs could also be used)   5.8

Required position (20   18.2 +   5.8)   20   24.0

2. Find the position of Mars at 6.00 pm GMT on March 4, 1965. As above, the difference for 6 hours, 1 minute sidereal time is 5.8

Subtract this from the noon position of Mars on March 4:

20   41.2 − 5.8   20   35.4

(Note that in the figures above seconds are given as decimal fractions of a minute)

In an ephemeris table all the times following the symbol R are retrograde until D (for "direct") appears in the column – this marks the turning point when the planet has resumed or will resume direct motion.

FORECASTING THE FUTURE

Astrology uses transits and progressions as time-tables for the future. Transits are movements of the planets which are indicated by formulae such as T♃ ♂ ☿, meaning, 'transiting Jupiter in conjunction with Mercury.' The transit is interpreted according to whether the planets are within the orb of conjunction and advancing towards its completion or moving away from each other after total concurrence, the former indicating an increasing interaction of both planets' potencies, the other their diminishing. There are also certain key-spots, the ascendant and the MC for example, on which planets are said to exert greater influence as they pass over them. Astrologers claim that times of opportunity or menace in a life can be indicated by a comparison of planet transits on a day years ahead, obtained from an ephemeris, with the position of the heavenly bodies on the natal chart. The type of event to be expected may also be indicated. One can see a promise or threat approaching, watch it happening and observe it modifying,

like weather systems on a film. An astrological principle is that the natal horoscope must never be contradicted, nor can one ever certainly foretell how an individual will react to promised wealth or threatened woe.

The student looking for future trends consults an ephemeris for the relevant day and notes the aspect of every planet in turn with each natal planet. Next, he notes the relationships of the transiting planets with the houses – in the case of fast-moving planets as accurately as possible by interpolation – and then summarizes his findings.

Progressions are daily positions of the planets after the day of birth plotted according to a formula of 'a day for a year'. The positions of planets and signs twenty days after a birth allegedly give an approximation of trends occurring in the subject's twentieth year, thirty days after of happenings in the thirtieth year, etc. Progressions are calculated proportionately, one day to a year, 12 hours to six months, one hour to 15 days, four minutes to one day and one minute to six hours. For exact work, calculate in days.

For the many who do not know their hour of birth, a 'flat'

EXAMPLE: Forecast the astrological conditions at midday on 27th June, 1991, for a subject born at 14.53 on 13th October, 1963

	YEARS	MONTHS	DAYS	HOURS	MINUTES
Hours and minutes after the birth on 13th October until midnight				9	7
Days from 13th until end of October			18		
Months from October till end of 1963		2			
Years from 1964 to 1990	27				
Months in 1991 till end of May		5			
Days till 26th June			26		
Hours on 27th June till midday				12	
TOTAL	27	8	14	21	7
(30 days from the 'Days' column are carried forward as 1 Month)					

Progression Calculations 27 years = 27 days; 8 months = 16 hours; 14 days = 1 hour, 56 minutes; 21 hours = 3½ minutes; 7 minutes is too small to be included.

Total: 27 days, 18 hours to the nearest hour. Adding 27 days 18 hours to the birth time we arrive at 08.53 on 10th November, when the sky will approximate to that

at noon on 27th June, 1991. (A calculation on a basis of 10,119 days between the above dates divided by 365¼, allowing for Leap Years, gives exactly the same result)

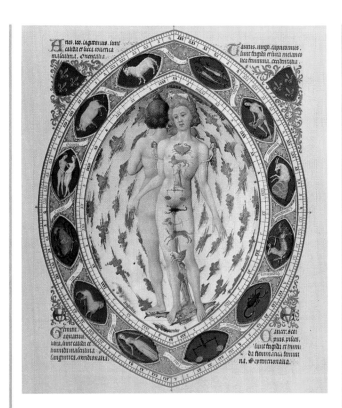

THE HOUSES

There are at least nine systems of plotting the divisions of the houses in a chart. A serious student of astrology needs to know them and the reasonings and calculations behind each and should study a specialist publication such as *House Systems Comparison*, which lists house cusps and gives the placement of the planets according to each system.

THE SIGNS

There are also differences in the spaces given to the signs which expand and contract according to their positions in the zodiac. The latitudes of the rising and setting of heavenly bodies are determined by the earth's tilt; from this arises the concept of signs of long ascension and short ascension, whereby some signs take longer to rise than others.

The simplest method is to use 30° divisions for both houses and signs, which provides horoscopes as adequate as those erected by other systems. The advanced student must, however, study every method and choose that which seems to him most accurate and effective.

TOP A zodiac from *Les Tres Riches Heures du Duc De Berry* showing the influence of the different constellations on the parts of the body.

LEFT An engraving showing Arab astrologers using early astronomical instruments.

BELOW An astrological chart of the northern hemisphere, showing the constellations, from the beautifully illustrated *Atlas Coelistis* of Andreas Cellarius.

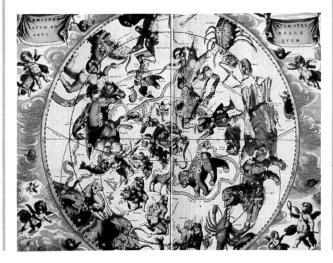

chart may be drawn with 0° Aries at the ascendant and the planets placed at their noon positions on the birthday. This is too approximate to be satisfactory. The astrologer may make two or more calculations based on different times on the birthday and decide which of them suits his subject's character best, but this method is too subjective. A better way, known as 'rectification' is to erect a horoscope for the dates and times of great events in the subject's life (marriage, grave illness, change of career) and see which birth chart fits them best.

CHAPTER TWO

THE SIGNS OF THE ZODIAC

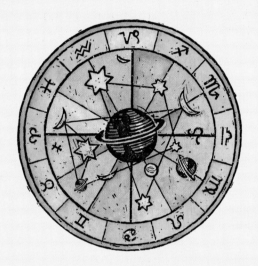

For the purposes of brevity, the masculine pronoun has been
used throughout, wherever comments apply to both male and
female subjects.

† ARIES †

The spring equinox, March 21, is the beginning of the zodiacal year and Aries, the first sign, is therefore that of new beginnings. The young ram is adventurous, ambitious, impulsive, enthusiastic and full of energy. He is a pioneer both in thought and action, very open to new ideas and a lover of freedom. He welcomes challenges and will not be diverted from his purpose except by his own impatience, which will surface if he doesn't get quick results.

Aries subjects are courageous leaders with a genuine concern for those they command, but they will not hesitate to use their subordinates to obtain their own objectives as leaders. As followers they can be troublesome, for they are apt to be immoderate in action and expression. They may be

RIGHT Charles (Charlie) Spencer Chaplin (1889–1977), born April 16. His work in the new art-form of the cinema had the pioneer quality associated with Aries.

LEFT Aries, from an English Psalter, York, c1170.

RIGHT Marlon Brando, born April 3 1924, shows Arien qualities in many of the roles he plays – energy, courage and determination, and something of a macho image.

PHYSICAL ATTRIBUTES

ABOVE Adolf Hitler (1889–1945), born April 20.

Physically Ariens are moderate in height and girth, inclined to spareness, but strong boned and with sturdy limbs. A long head surmounting a long neck sits on often stout shoulders. The complexion tends to be dark, even swarthy. They are apt to be heavy sleepers because of the exhausting pace at which they lead their lives.

unwilling to obey or submit to directions for which they can see no reason, or with which they disagree. They are much concerned with self, both positively and negatively – self-reliant but also self-centred – and concerned with their own personal advancement and physical satisfaction to the point of greed. Their immense energy makes them aggressive and restless, argumentative, headstrong, quick tempered, easily offended and capable of holding grudges if they feel themselves affronted. Thus, if at work superiors cooperate well with their Aries employees, approving of their good qualities, they will receive from them complete loyalty; but if an Arien considers himself unappreciated or exploited, he is likely to give notice impulsively, to nurse resentment and even, in extreme cases, to revenge himself by slandering his former firm, or by acts of sabotage.

In their personal relationships Ariens are frank, direct and candid, and make enthusiastic and generous friends. They are liable to have a high sex drive and make passionate

ABOVE An illustration of an Arien subject from a 16th-century Turkish treatise on Astrology. Perhaps the severed head implies immoderateness in action!

but fastidious lovers. There is, however, a negative side to their associations with other people. They can be easily irritated by slowness or moderation in their companions and, though themselves sensitive, ride roughshod over the sensitivities of others. The intensity of their sexual urges can drive them to promiscuity and a Don Juan-like counting of conquests of the opposite sex. It can also trick them into early unwise marriage which may end disastrously. Their love of change more than counters the little loyalty they have, and their tenacity, though sufficient to achieve short-term objects, is unlikely to stand up to the challenge of a lifetime's faithfulness. They can be brusque, rude, bullying, even brutal and immature, and were summed up by Lilly, an early astrologer, as "bestial, luxurious, intemperate and violent."

Mentally Ariens are intellectual and objective, but can be bigoted and extremist in religion and politics. They are good champions of lost causes and last-ditch resistance. They are quick-witted but foolhardy and over-optimistic, lacking thoroughness and the ability to evaluate difficulties in the undertakings into which they often rush impulsively. The great need of the Aries native is to exercise an iron self-control, to discipline the qualities and tendencies of his character to the advantage, not the detriment, of the society in which he moves.

They can make good athletes and climbers, doctors, explorers (of new ideas as well as uncharted territory, the latter in these days including adventuring into outer space), soldiers, sailors and airmen, especially in circumstances which demand the "Nelson touch," and leaders – though awkward subordinates – in industry and politics.

Aries governs the head and brain, and Ariens are said to be prone to headaches, particularly migraines, sunstroke, neuralgia and depression. Indigestion and nervous disorders are also threats to them, and their rashness, impetuosity and wholesale physical commitment make them liable to accidents and physical injuries.

FAMOUS ARIENS

Bette Davis (1908–1989), born April 5. Miss Davis displayed the Arien qualities of tenacity, self confidence and energy.

Severiano Ballesteros, born April 9, 1957. Considered by some to be the world's number one golfer; Ariens make good athletes.

Henry James (1843–1916), born April 15. American-British novelist and critic, one of the most influential literary figures of his day. His awesome intellectual abilities can be seen as an Arien trait: his hypochondria and general lack of physical drive cannot.

Thomas Jefferson (1743–1826) born April 13. The 3rd President of the United States, whose tremendous range of interests and activities exhibit the immense energy of some Ariens.

† TAURUS †

Physically the Taurean is a heavy, thickset type, sometimes hefty or even clumsy, and usually strong. He ranges from average to shorter than usual height, with broad shoulders, and tends to be slow walking and inclined to corpulence. He can give an impression of awkwardness and clumsiness on the one hand, because his breadth seems disproportionate to his height, but on the other he can be extremely dignified and majestically good-looking. His features often include a broad forehead, large, well-set eyes, an aquiline nose, a wide mouth with thick lips, set in a swarthy face with heavy jaws and thick black or sandy hair, often coarse and curling. He is usually strong not only in body but in personality.

RIGHT This Taurus subject, from a 16th-century Turkish treatise, exhibits the love of music of some born under the sign by the lyre which he is carrying.

LEFT Fred Astaire (1899–1985), born May 10. American dancer and film star, physically untypical of a Taurus subject but with talent for his particular art, that of dancing, not far short of genius.

His characteristics are solidity, practicality, extreme determination and strength of will – no one will ever drive him, but he will willingly and loyally follow a leader whom he trusts. He is stable, balanced, conservative – a good, law-abiding citizen and a lover of peace, possessing all the best qualities of the bourgeoisie. As he has a sense of material values and physical possessions, respect for property and a horror of falling into debt, he will do everything in his power to maintain the security of the *status quo* and may be stupidly hostile to change.

ABOVE William Shakespeare (1564–1616), baptized April 26. Shakespeare could just have been born under Aries rather than Taurus, though baptism then followed as soon as possible after birth.

ABOVE Sigmund Freud (1856–1939), born May 6, the Father of modern psychology. Freud was, on the whole, an untypical Taurean. Perhaps a waspish Jungian would point to the Taurean characteristics of obstinacy and self-righteousness.

He is a faithful and generous friend with a great capacity for affection, but rarely makes friends with anyone outside his own social rank, to which he is normally excessively faithful. In the main, he is gentle, even-tempered, good-natured, modest and slow to anger, disliking quarreling and avoiding ill-feeling. If he is provoked, however, he can explode into violent outbursts of ferocious anger in which he seems to lose all self-control. Equally unexpected are his occasional sallies into humour and exhitions of fun.

If anyone offends his *amour propre* he can be a determined enemy, though magnanimous in forgiveness if his opponent makes an effort to meet him halfway.

He is more than averagely amorous and sensually self-conscious, but sexually straightforward and not given to experiment. He makes a constant, faithful, home-loving husband and a thoughtful, kindly father, demanding too much neither of his wife nor his children. He can be over-possessive and he may sometimes play the game of engineering family rows for the pleasure of making up the quarrel.

Although his physical appearance may appear to belie it, he has a strong aesthetic taste, enjoying art, for which he may have a talent, beauty (actively recoiling from anything sordid or ugly) and music. He may have a strong, sometimes unconventional, religious faith. Allied to his taste for all things beautiful is a love for the physical good things of life – pleasure, comfort, luxury and good food and wine – and he may have to resist the temptation to over-indulgence, leading to drunkenness, gross sensuality, and covetousness.

Mentally, he is keen-witted and practical rather than intellectual, but apt to become fixed in his opinions through his preference for following accepted and reliable patterns of experience. His character generally is dependable, steadfast, prudent, just, firm and unshaken in the face of difficulties. His vices arise from his virtues, going to extremes such as being too slavish to the conventions he admires, obstinately and exasperatingly self-righteous, an unoriginal, rigid, ultra-conservative, argumentative, querulous bore, stuck in a self-centred rut. He may develop a brooding resentment through nursing a sense of injuries received and, whether his character is positive or negative, he needs someone to stroke his ego with a frequent, "Well done!"

Taurus governs the throat and neck and its subjects need to beware of throat infections, goitre and respiratory ailments such as asthma. They are said to be at risk of diseases of the genitals, womb, liver and kidneys, and of abscesses and rheumatism. Because their bodily type has an inclination to physical laziness, Taureans can be overweight.

WORK

ABOVE Barbara Streisand, born April 24, 1942. American actress and singer.

In his work the Taurean is industrious and a good handcraftsman, and is not afraid of getting his hands dirty. He is reliable, practical, methodical and ambitious, within a framework of obedience to superiors. He is at his best in routine positions of trust and responsibility, where there is little need of urgency and even less risk of change, and a pension at the end. Yet he is creative and a good founder of enterprises where the rewards of his productiveness come from his own work and not that of others. He can flourish in many different trades and professions: banking, accountancy, architecture, building, almost any form of bureaucracy, auctioneering, farming, medicine, chemistry, industry – Taureans make good managers and foremen – surveying, insurance, education and, perhaps surprisingly, music and sculpture. He makes an ideal trustee or guardian, and can attain eminence as a chef. Some Taureans are gifted enough in singing to become opera stars or to excel in more popular types of music, like Streisand.

†GEMINI†

Gemini, the sign of the Twins, is dual-natured, elusive, complex and contradictory. On the one hand it produces the virtue of versatility, and on the other the vices of two-facedness and flightiness. The sign is linked with Mercury, the planet of childhood and youth, and its subjects tend to have the graces and faults of the young. When they are good, they are very attractive; when they are bad they are all the more horrible for being the charmers that they are. Like children they are lively, happy – if circumstances are right for them – egocentric, imaginative and restless. They take up new activities enthusiastically but lack application, constantly needing new interests, flitting from project to project as apparently purposelessly as a butterfly dancing from flower to flower. To them life is a game which must always be full of fresh moves and continuous entertainment, free of labour and routine.

Since they lack the quality of conscientiousness, they are apt to fight a losing battle in any attempts they make to be moral (in the widest sense of the word). Their good qualities are attractive and come easily to them. They are affectionate, courteous, kind, generous, and thoughtful towards the poor and suffering – provided none of the activities resulting from expressing these traits interferes too greatly with their own lives and comforts. They quickly learn to use their outward attractiveness to gain their own ends, and when striving for these they will use any weapon in their armoury – unscrupulous lying, cunning evasiveness – escaping blame by contriving to put it on other people, wrapped up in all the charm they can turn on. In their better moments they may strive to be honest and straightforward, but self-interest is almost always the victor. If things go against them, they sulk like children. Also like children, they demand attention, admiration and the spending on them of time, energy and money, throwing tantrums if they don't get what they want. They reflect every change in their surroundings, like chameleons, and can become pessimistic, sullen, peevish and materialistically self-

INTELLECT

ABOVE Thomas Hardy (1840–1928), born June 2. The English novelist and poet shows the two-sidedness of Gemini in, for example, his sombre novels and lyrical poetry.

Geminians have a keen, intuitive, sometimes brilliant intelligence and they love cerebral challenges. But their concentration, though intense for a while, does not last. Their mental agility and energy give them a voracious appetite for knowledge from youth onward, though they dislike the labour of learning. They easily grasp almost everything requiring intelligence and mental dexterity and are often able to marry manual skill to their qualities of mind. Their intellect is strongly analytical and sometimes gives them so great an ability to see both sides of a question that they vacillate and find it hard to take decisions. But their intelligence may very well be used to control and unify the duality of their natures into a most efficient unit. If faced with difficulties, they have little determination to worry at a problem until they find a solution – they will pick the brains of others. In their intellectual pursuits, as in other departments of their lives, they risk becoming dilettantes, losing themselves in too many projects which they follow until they become difficult.

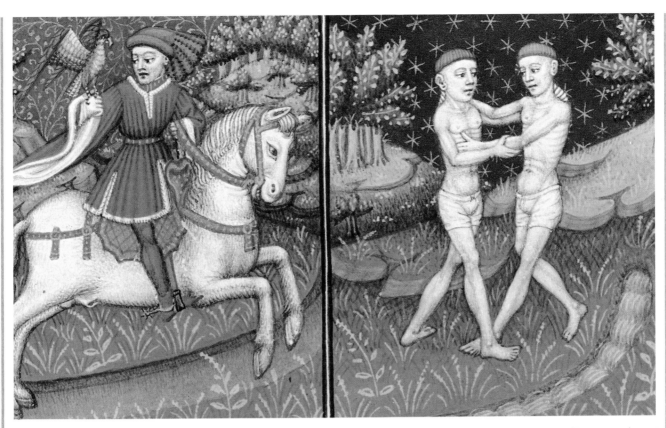

ABOVE A mid-15th-century French illustration of Gemini. Falconry was a summer sport and its depiction here simply indicates the time of year, not some Geminian qualities.

RIGHT H.R.H. Philip, Duke of Edinburgh, born June 10, 1921. This photograph of the laughing Duke pictures the happy side of the Geminian character.

centred if circumstances force them to struggle in any way. If the conditions of life become really adverse, their strength of will may desert them entirely. They can become uncertain of themselves, either withdrawn or nervously excitable worriers, sullenly discontented, hard and irritable, with "Self" looming ever larger in their struggles. On the other hand their versatility can make them very adaptable, adjusting themselves to control the world around them by means of their inherent ingenuity and cleverness.

In love they are fickle, not intentionally so but because of the basic inconsistency of their emotional nature, which has an amoral aspect to it. There is a side to Geminians which can become deeply involved emotionally, and another, hostile to sentimentality, which stands back from a romantic situation,

RIGHT Marilyn Monroe (1926–1962), born June 1. Her character and career exemplified many of the Geminian traits, though it may be said that her virtues were her own and her misfortunes imposed upon her by circumstances. Her stars illustrate the mystery surrounding her death.

laughing at it and the protagonists in it, including themselves, and analyzes it intellectually. Gemini subjects take nothing seriously. So, in love, in spite of their temporary depth of feeling — for the intensity of involvement lasts only while it is new — they are superficial, light-hearted, cool, flirtatious and unimaginative in the understanding of the pain they may give others. They like intrigue, the excitement of the chase, but once they have caught the prey, they lose interest and look around for the next creature to pursue. In less serious situations they make witty, entertaining companions, good acquaintances rather than friends. Even at their worst they are never dull — there is usually playfulness below the surface, and they can be brilliant conversationalists — but they can also be quarrelsome, prattlers, boasters, liars and cheats.

Geminians can be successful in many walks of life though their general characters tend to make them unreliable. They are often skillful manipulators of language, in speech and writing, and may be debaters, diplomats (though in politics they are more interested in theory than practice), orators, preachers (brilliant rather than profound), teachers, authors and poets, journalists or lawyers. In business any work which combines quick-wittedness with change of surroundings suits them — working as a travelling salesman, brokerage work or dealing of any kind. Because they are dispassionate, logical, rational and analytical they make good scientists, especially medically, astronomers and mathematicians. They can also make excellent members of the Forces, for they take danger no more seriously than anything else and can earn themselves a reputation for devotion to duty and heroic acts. In the arts they may excel in music, painting and sculpture. They make good psychical researchers of a sceptical kind. Negatively they can degenerate into confidence tricksters, thieves and even adepts in the black arts.

Physically Geminians often appear youthful, even child-like. They have tall, thin, but strong and active, bodies, with long arms and legs culminating in short, fleshy hands and feet. Their faces are also inclined to be long and sallow, with large, piercing hazel eyes, often in contrast with dark complexions. Their hair is often dark, almost black. They use their eyes and hands expressively — they are great gesticulators — and their movements are quick and active.

Gemini rules the arms, shoulders, hands, lungs and nervous system and its subjects need to beware of diseases and accidents associated with the upper part of the body, as well as nervous and pulmonary disorders such as catarrh and bronchitis. Their mercurial nature may also affect a constitution which is usually not strong if it is put under strain.

ABOVE Sir Arthur Conan Doyle (1859–1930), born May 22. A many-sided character, he was active in public affairs, the creator of the astute, practical Sherlock Holmes, and a convinced Spiritualist.

† CANCER †

The Cancerian character is the least clear-cut of all those associated with the signs of the zodiac. It can range from the timid, dull, shy and withdrawn to the most brilliant, and famous Cancerians are to be found throughout the whole range of human activity. It is a fundamentally conservative and home-loving nature, appreciating the nestlike quality of a secure base to which the male can retire when he needs respite from the stresses of life, and in which the Cancerian woman can exercise her strong maternal instincts. The latter tends to like and to have a large family. "Nestlike" is an appropriate adjective for the Cancerian home, for its inhabitants tend to favour the dark, mysterious, but comfortable type of house which has something of the air of a den about it, a place which belongs to the family rather than existing as a showcase to impress visitors.

That is not to say that the Cancerian is unsociable, just that for him there is a time to socialize and a time to be solitary, and this is part of the apparent contradiction in his nature. Outwardly he can appear formidable – thick-skinned, unemotional, uncompromising, obstinately tenacious, purposeful, energetic, shrewd, intuitive and wise, sometimes with a philosophical profundity of thought verging on inspiration. His intimates, however, may see a very different character, one with a sympathetic and kindly sensitivity to other people, especially those he loves. He is able to identify with the situations of others because of the keenness of his imagination. He is often over-imaginative and prone to fantasy, sometimes trying to shape his life to fit some romantic ideal. He is appreciative of art and literature, and especially of drama, where the spectacle and ebb and flow of action and feeling particularly excite him. He may himself possess considerable literary, artistic or oratorical talent. His sharp ear and talent for mimicry can sometimes give him success on the stage, though his tendency to be emotional may make him overact. Interestingly – because he gives the impression of being down-to-earth – he is often fascinated by the occult and

is more open to psychic influence than the average. If he can reconcile the personal conflict of his urge to be outgoing with the reserve that causes him to withdraw into himself, then at his best he can inspire his generation, especially the youthful part of it, by his idealism. A job in which he could express this, and in which he could do well, would be as a leader in a youth organization.

In his personal relationships he is mentally a mixture of toughness and softness, often emotional and romantic to the point of sentimentality in his fantasies; but in real life and in his marriage, his loving is not sentimental but tenaciously loyal. Even if he has affairs (and he may do so, for the male in particular is open to sensual stimulation), his first loyalty remains to his wife and family, of whom he regards himself as the protector. Both the Cancerian man and woman love unreservedly, giving much and asking little in return – in fact one of the most important lessons they have to learn is to receive gracefully. They are too easily influenced by those

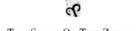

OPPOSITE Mike Tyson is an example of (in his own field) the "most brilliant" of Cancerians, and he is certainly "outwardly formidable," though not perhaps in the usual meaning of the term for the Cancer subject.

ABOVE This mid-fifteenth century French illustration of Cancer the Crab is rather more like a lobster. The reaper again represents an activity of the season, not of the sign.

they love or admire, and swayed by the emotion of the moment. They are also loyal friends, the negative side of their faithfulness being clannishness, the narrow patriotism of "my country right or wrong"; and closing ranks in suspicion and coldness towards outsiders.

Cancerians have a retentive memory, particularly for emotionally laden events which they can recall in detail for years afterwards. They are strongly governed by childhood memories and, since they live intensely in the past in memory and in the future in imagination, a chance meeting with someone for whom they had unrequited love, even if they thought they had conquered the feeling, will easily rouse the emotion all over again.

His abilities fit the Cancerian for a wide range of occupations. As he is interested in what people are thinking and able to judge what they can safely be told, he can be a good journalist, writer or politician, though in this last capacity he is more likely to remain in the background rather than attain prominent positions of power. He may, indeed, change his party. He can serve in other departments of public affairs, especially those which involve looking after others, for example in any kind of service from welfare and nursing to catering – his own love of comfort and good living makes the Cancerian an excellent chef or housekeeper. He sometimes has a penchant for trade or business and is often successful as a captain of industry. This is because he is an excellent organizer with a good sense of value and economy which he may combine with a flair for inventiveness and originality. The romantic side of his nature makes him enjoy grubbing about in places where exciting discoveries may be made (old stamp collections in attics in which there may be a twopenny-blue Mauritius worth thousands of pounds!), and if he can do this professionally as a secondhand dealer or specialist in antiques, he will be happy. More common occupations which suit some subjects of Cancer are an estate agent, gardener and sailor.

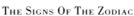

MARCI 10
ITE IN MVDVM VNIVIRSV ET PREDICATE
EVANGELIVM OMNI CREATVRE

FAULTS

The Cancerian has many potential faults. He can be untidy, sulky, devious, moody, inclined to self-pity because of an inferiority complex, broods on insults (very often imagined), yet is easily flattered. He can be tactless and difficult yet, because he is normally ambitious, he will curry favour by floating with the majority opinions, outlook and fashions of the day. As a result he often changes his opinions and loyalties and, indeed, his occupations, and lacks stability. He is easily corrupted and, because he is a convincing romanticizer, can make a successful confidence trickster. His romanticism in another sense makes him an ardent supporter of causes, for example of a football team with whose heroes he can identify in a world of fantasy.

Gaius Julius Caesar (100–44 BC) should be included among the Cancerians illustrated, for the greater number of them are born in July, to which the name of the Roman month, Quinctilis, was changed in his honour.

OPPOSITE Henry VIII (1491–1547), born June 28. Here was a man in whom many of the Cancerian virtues and vices are to be found. Consider, to begin with, the physical attributes assigned to the Cancerian, described below.

RIGHT H.R.H. the Princess of Wales, born July 1, 1961, appears to belong to the naturally shy and private group of Cancerians, but has been forced by circumstances to be always in the limelight.

Physically he is average to below average in height, with a fleshy body and short legs in comparison with the rest of him. His hair is usually brown, his face round, his complexion pale, his forehead prominent, his eyes small and blue or grey in colour, his nose short, perhaps upturned, and his mouth full. He sometimes walks clumsily.

Cancer governs the chest, breasts, elbows, stomach and digestion, womb and female reproductive organs. Cancer, which can affect any part of the body, is sometimes said to have taken its name from this sign, which can therefore afflict its subjects with imperfections anywhere. This is incorrect, however, the derivation of cancer being the Latin *cancer* meaning gangrene as well as crab. Nevertheless, Cancerians are said to be liable to breast cancer and to suffer from pleurisy, dropsy, piles and varicose veins. The excitability mentioned above can lead to weak digestion, gastritis and other stomach ills, and there is a tendency to coughs and weakness of vision.

† LEO †

The Leo type is the most dominant, spontaneously creative and extrovert of all the zodiacal characters. In grandeur of manner, splendour of bearing and magnanimity of personality, he is the monarch among humans as the lion is king of the beasts. He is ambitious, courageous, dominant, strong willed, positive, independent, self-confident – there is no such word as doubt in his vocabulary – and self-controlled. A born leader, either in support of or in revolt against the *status quo*, he is at his most effective when in a position of command, his personal magnetism and courtesy of mind bringing out the

best of loyalty from his subordinates. As he is uncomplicated, knowing exactly what he wants and using all his energy, creativeness and resolution to get it, as well as being certain that he will, his followers know where they are with him. Although the ambitiousness of his schemes and idealism may sometimes daunt them, for he thinks and acts bigger than would normally be dared, his practical hard-headedness and ability to go straight to the heart of any problem reassures them. If he meets with setbacks he thrives on the adversity.

On the whole he is a power for good, for he is strongly idealistic, humane and beneficent. He has a powerful intelligence and is of a broad, philosophical, sometimes religious, turn of mind. If he is devout, he may become very obstinate in upholding traditional beliefs and will cling tenaciously, but with complete sincerity, to practices and doctrines which liberal thinkers regard as absurdly out-of-date.

His faults can be as large in scale as his virtues, and an excessively negative Leonian can be one of the most unpleasant human beings imaginable, displaying extreme arrogance, autocratic pride, haughtiness and excessive hastiness of temper. If jealously suspicious of rivals, he will not hesitate

BELOW Conventionally in heraldy and other symbolic representations of the lion, the creature is shown, as here, with an almost human face.

RIGHT Napoleon I (1769–1821), Emperor of France, born August 15. He was in his career an exemplar of what a Leo should be, perhaps above all, in the ability to elicit loyalty from his followers.

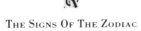

RIGHT George Bernard Shaw (1856–1950), born July 26. A man who strode magisterially through the world of letters, pouring scorn on rivals and critics alike, another Leo whose single-mindedness in his chosen career brought him fame and success.

to use cunning, lies and trickery to discredit them. Self-centredness, greed for flattery, boastfulness and bombast, pomposity, snobbish superiority, and overbearing and intolerant disdain of underlings – to whom he will nevertheless delegate the carrying out of minor details in his grandiose schemes, and from whom he is not above borrowing immoderately if an occasion necessitates it – any of these can be characteristic of him. Add to them a passion for luxury, a lust for power, unlimited sexual lust and emotional indulgence, and a character emerges that no one would want to know either in public life or in private. But his pride may go before a fall as uncontrolled impetuosity is likely to bring him low. Fortunately it is rare that a Leo is so undisciplined as to give way thoroughly to this list of vices, and his tendencies to them are usually more than balanced by his innate wisdom.

In his professional life he does well in any vocation at which there is room at the top. As a politician he will be content with nothing less than a powerful position in government. In business he will be chairman of his company's board, or at least a director or manager. He is an excellent organizer and overseer, and if from the artisan ranks of society he will aspire to become the boss, partly because his nature is to be ambitious, partly because he dislikes manual labour preferring to take charge of others doing it. If artistic, Leos can become stars of stage or screen (their bent is serious rather than light drama), maestros as musicians – when they will gravitate toward the grand instruments or activities, such as the organ or conducting of orchestras – and as painters; anything grand in conception and scale appeals to them. Leo women especially make good social workers.

Physically Leos have large, strong and active bodies, broad shouldered, big boned, taller than average, yet narrow flanked and often lean in youth. Such physiques often run to plumpness as the years pass (though usually majestically so!). Their heads are large and round, their hair usually blond and curly, their complexions florid, their expression imperious. The eyes, often blue or grey, are wide, prominent and keen. They stride masterfully and in a stately fashion, their upright carriage reflecting the sense that they have a right to be here.

Physiologically, Leo governs the upper back, forearms, wrists, spine and heart. Its natives are subject to a number of ailments: pains in the back and lungs, spinal complaints, diseases of the heart and blood, sickness in ribs and sides, convulsions, pleurisies, violent burning fevers – including, in former days when they were prevalent, plague and pestilence – jaundice and some afflictions of the eyes.

PERSONAL RELATIONSHIPS

ABOVE Mae West (1893–1980), born August 17. American film actress, famous for her openly flaunted (but wonderfully respectable) sexuality.

In his (or her) relations with others the Leo type is open, sincere, genuine and trusting. Outgoing, spontaneously warm hearted and plain spoken, though never lacking in kindliness, he is more disillusioned than the average if those he trusts let him down. He is not a good judge of character and is inclined to favouritism and an exaggerated faith in his followers that too often ends in disappointment. He has a strong sex drive and is so easily attracted to the opposite sex that he finds it hard to be constant; he can be so intensely sexual as to become dissolute. He may have numerous love affairs for his love of pleasure and beauty is liable to drive him from one attractive partner to another. He is very much inclined to be a deceiver. His marriage may fail for the same reason, yet he is sincere and generous to his lovers while love lasts, and he will remain attached to his home so long as it is run for his benefit. He demands service but is incapable of giving it.

† VIRGO †

Virgo is the only zodiacal sign represented by a female. It is sometimes thought of as a potentially creative girl, delicately lovely; sometimes as a somewhat older woman, intelligent but rather pedantic and spinsterish. The latter impression is sometimes confirmed by the Virgoan preciseness, refinement, fastidious love of cleanliness, hygiene and good order, conventionality and aristocratic attitude of reserve. They are usually observant, shrewd, critically inclined, judicious, patient, practical supporters of the *status quo*, and tend towards conservatism in all departments of life. On the surface they are emotionally cold, and sometimes this goes deeper, for their habit of suppressing their natural kindness may in the end cause it to atrophy, with the result that they shrink from committing themselves to friendship, make few relationships, and those they do make they are careful to keep superficial. But the outward lack of feeling may, in some individuals born under this sign, conceal too much emotion, to which they are afraid of giving way because they do not trust others, nor do they have confidence in themselves and their judgments. This is because they are conscious of certain shortcomings in themselves – of worldliness, of practicality, of sophistication and of outgoingness. So they bring the art of self-concealment to a high pitch, hiding their apprehensiveness about themselves and their often considerable sympathy with other people under a mantle of matter-of-factness and undemonstrative, quiet reserve. They are still waters that run deep. Yet in their unassuming, outwardly

BELOW Here Virgo is symbolized as a young girl, in her left hand a palm-branch, her right hand raised in blessing – or admonition!

OPPOSITE Lauren Bacall, born September 16, 1924, American film actress. It is always difficult to discern the private person behind the mask created by the media, but many of the Virgoan qualities seem to belong here.

cheerful and agreeable fashion, they can be sensible, discreet, well spoken, wise and witty, with a good understanding of other people's problems which they can tackle with a practicality not always evident in their own personal relationships.

Both sexes have considerable charm and dignity, which makes some male Virgoans appear effeminate when they are not. In marriage they can be genuinely affectionate, making good spouses and parents, but their love-making is a perfection of technique rather than the expression of desire, and they must be careful not to mate with a partner whose sex drive requires a passion they cannot match.

They are intellectually enquiring, methodical and logical, studious and teachable. They combine mental ingenuity with the ability to produce a clear analysis of the most complicated problems. They have an excellent eye for detail but they may be so meticulous that they neglect larger issues. Also, although they are realists, they may slow down projects by being too exact. They are practical with their hands, good technicians and have genuine inventive talents. Thoroughness, hard

RIGHT Elizabeth I (1533–1603), Queen of England, born September 7. She was, as the Virgin Queen, appropriately a native of Virgo, although, uncharacteristically, a leader rather than a follower.

CONSTITUTION

Virgo is said to govern the hands, abdomen, intestines, spleen and central nervous system. Illnesses to which its natives are prone include catarrh, colds, coughs, pleurisies, pneumonia and nervous instability. Their natures incline them to worry and this makes them vulnerable to stomach and bowel troubles, including colic and ulcers. Male Virgoans may have trouble with their sexual organs. Both sexes are strongly interested in drugs and esoteric cuisine and as their delicate stomachs require them to be careful about their diet, it is essential that they treat their fascination with exotic food with extreme care.

LEFT Michael Jackson (b. 1958), probably the highest-paid performing artist in the world today. Certainly a perfectionist, arguably a hypochondriac.

work and conscientiousness are their hallmarks, and they are such perfectionists that, if things go wrong, they are easily discouraged. Because of their ability to see every angle of a many-sided question, they are unhappy with abstract theorizing. Appreciating the many different points of view as they do, they find philosophical concepts difficult, and they vacillate and have no confidence in any conclusions at which they arrive.

With these qualities, they are better as subordinates than leaders. Responsibility irks them and they often lack the breadth of strategic vision that a leader needs – Virgoans are essentially tacticians, admirable in the attainment of limited objectives. Their self-distrust is something they project on to other people and tends to make them exacting employers, though in the demands they make on those under them they temper this attitude with justice. They have potential abilities in the arts, sciences and languages. Language especially they use correctly, clearly, concisely and formally, as grammarians and etymologists rather than for their literary interests, yet they are likely to have a good memory for apt quotations. Although they are well suited for careers in machine-drawing, surveying and similar occupations, they are better fitted for a job in a library or office than a workshop. Their minds are such that they need the stimulus of practical problems to be solved rather than the mere routine or working to set specifications that need no thought. They are careful with money and their interest in statistics makes them excellent bookkeepers and accountants. They also make good editors, physicists and analytical chemists. They may also find success as social workers, ministering to those less fortunate than themselves. They can be doctors, nurses, psychologists, teachers, confidential secretaries, technologists, inspectors, musicians, critics, public speakers, and writers – especially of reference works such as dictionaries and encyclopedias. Both sexes have a deep interest in history, a feature recognized by astrological authorities for at least two hundred years. If they go in for a business career their shrewdness and analytical ingenuity could tempt them into dishonesty, though they usually have enough moral sense to resist temptation. Female Virgoans may find a career in fashion, for they have a flair for dress, in which they can be trendsetters. In any profession they choose the natives of this sign readily assimilate new ideas, but always with caution, conserving what they consider worth keeping from the past. They love country life but are unlikely to make good farmers, unless they can contrive to carry out their work without outraging their sense of hygiene and cleanliness.

Their faults, as is usual with all zodiacal types, are the extremes of their virtues. Fastidious reticence and modesty become old-maidishness and pernicketiness; balanced criticism becomes carping and nagging; and concern for detail becomes over-specialization. Virgoans are liable to indecision in wider issues and this can become chronic, turning molehills of minor difficulties into Himalayas of crisis. Their prudence can become guile and their carefulness, turned in on themselves, can produce worriers and hypochondriacs.

Physically they are above average height, their bodies slender but compact and well proportioned, often with dark hair and eyes. Their complexions are ruddy or brown and their faces oval. The men are not classically handsome but are well favoured and attractive, the women good looking and winsome, often lovely but not stereotypical beauties. Both sexes use language well, though their voices are inclined to be small and shrill.

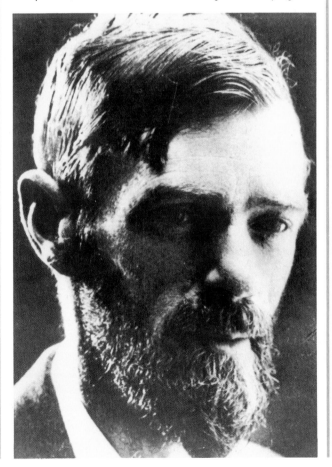

BELOW David Herbert Lawrence (1885–1930) born September 11, English novelist and poet. There is a feminine streak in some of his writing that is markedly Virgoan.

† LIBRA †

Libra is the only inanimate sign of the zodiac, all the others representing either humans or animals. Many modern astrologers regard it as the most desirable of zodiacal types because it represents the zenith of the year, the high point of the seasons, when the harvest of all the hard work of the spring is reaped. There is a mellowness and sense of relaxation in the air as mankind enjoys the last of the summer sun and the fruits of his toil. Librans too are among the most civilized of the twelve zodiacal characters and are often good looking. They have elegance, charm and good taste, are naturally kind, very gentle, and lovers of beauty, harmony (both in music and social living) and the pleasure that these bring.

They have a good critical faculty and are able to stand back and look impartially at matters which call for an impartial judgment to be made on them. But they do not tolerate argument with anyone who challenges their opinions, for once they have reached a conclusion, its truth seems to them self-evident; and among their faults is an impatience of criticism and a greed for approval. But their characters are on the whole balanced, diplomatic and even tempered.

Their cast of mind is artistic rather than intellectual, though they are usually too moderate and well balanced to be *avant garde* in any artistic endeavour. They have good perception and observation and their critical ability, with which they are able to view their own efforts as well as those of others, gives their work integrity.

In their personal relationships they show understanding of the other person's point of view, trying to resolve any differences by compromise, and are often willing to allow claims against themselves to be settled to their own disadvantage rather than spoil a relationship. They like the opposite sex to the extent of promiscuity sometimes, and may indulge in romanticism bordering on sentimentality. Their marriages, however, stand a good chance of success because they are frequently the union of "true minds." The Libran's continuing kindness toward his partner mollifies any hurt the latter

SOCIAL RELATIONSHIPS

ABOVE Mohandas Karamchanal Gandhi (1869–1948), born October 2. Architect of India's freedom, a Libran in his passion for justice and self-discipline in attaining his objects.

Librans are sensitive to the needs of others and have the gift, sometimes to an almost psychic extent, of understanding the emotional needs of their companions and meeting them with their own innate optimism – they are the kind of people of whom it is said, "They always make you feel better for having been with them." They are very sociable beings. They loathe cruelty, viciousness and vulgarity and detest conflict between people, so they do their best to cooperate and compromise with everyone around them, and their ideal for their own circle and for society as a whole is unity.

ABOVE Sarah Bernhardt (1844–1923), born October 22. This French actress, who performed throughout the world, was typically Libran in her successful theatre managements.

ABOVE Franz Liszt (1811–1886), born October 22. He is pictured playing the piano for the Imperial Family in Vienna. Librans may find success as composers.

may feel if the two have had a tiff. Nor can the Libran's spouse often complain that he or she is not understood, for the Libran is usually the most empathetic of all the zodiacal types and the most ready to tolerate the beloved's failings.

The negative Libran character may show frivolity, flirtatiousness and shallowness. It can be changeable and indecisive, impatient of routine, colourlessly conventional and timid, easygoing to the point of inertia, seldom angry when circumstances demand a show of annoyance at least; and yet Librans can shock everyone around them with sudden storms of rage. Their love of pleasure may lead them into extrava-

gance; Libran men can degenerate into reckless gamblers, and Libran women — extravagant, jealous and careless about money — sometimes squander their wealth and talents in their over-enthusiasm for causes which they espouse. Both sexes can become great gossipers. A characteristic of the type is an insatiable curiosity that tempts them to enquire into every social scandal in their circle.

In their work the description "lazy Libra" which is sometimes given is actually more alliterative than true. Librans can be surprisingly energetic, though it is true that they dislike coarse, dirty work. Although some are modestly content, others are extremely ambitious. With their dislike of extremes they make good diplomats but perhaps poor party politicians, for they are moderate in their opinions and able to see other points of view. They can succeed as administrators, lawyers (they have a strong sense of justice, which cynics might say could handicap them in a legal career), antique dealers, civil servants and bankers, for they are trustworthy in handling other people's money. Some Librans are gifted in fashion designing or in devising new cosmetics; others may find success as artists, composers, critics, writers, interior decorators, social workers or valuers, and they have an ability in the management of all sorts of public entertainment. Some work philanthropically for humanity with great self-discipline and significant results. Libran financiers sometimes make good speculators, for they have the optimism and ability to recover from financial crashes.

Physically the Libran has a well-proportioned, fundamentally strong physique of between average height and tall, and a round skull and face. The hair is often fair, smooth, and fine rather than curly; the complexion is good and the eyes often blue and very expressive.

RIGHT Bruce Springstein, born September 23, 1949. The Boss: a musician very different from Liszt but still a Libran!

Libra governs the lumbar region, lower back and kidneys. Its subjects must beware of weaknesses in the back, and lumbago, and they are susceptible to troubles in the kidneys and bladder, especially gravel and stone. They need to avoid over-indulgence in food and especially drink, for the latter can particularly harm the kidneys.

† SCORPIO †

Scorpians are the most intense, profound, powerful characters in the zodiac. Even when they appear self-controlled and calm there is a seething intensity of emotional energy under the placid exterior. They are like the volcano not far under the surface of a calm sea – it may burst into eruption at any moment. But more ordinary mortals who are particularly perceptive will be aware of the harnessed aggression, the immense forcefulness, magnetic intensity and often strangely hypnotic personality under the tranquil but watchful composure of the Scorpian. In conventional social gatherings they are pleasant to be with, thoughtful in conversation, dignified and reserved, yet affable and courteous, and they sometimes possess penetrating eyes which may make their shyer companions feel naked and defenceless before them.

In their everyday behaviour they give the appearance of being withdrawn from the centre of activity, yet those who know them will recognize the watchfulness that is part of their character. They need great self-discipline, because they are able to recognize the qualities in themselves that make them different from other humans, and to know that their utterly unconventional natures can be used for great good or great evil. Their tenacity and willpower are immense, their depth of character and passionate conviction overwhelming, yet they are deeply sensitive and easily moved by their emotions. Their sensitivity, together with a propensity for extreme likes and dislikes, make them easily hurt, quick to detect insult or injury to themselves (often when none is intended) and easily aroused to ferocious anger. This may express itself in such destructive speech or action that they make life-long enemies by their outspokenness, for they find it difficult not to be over-critical of anything or anyone to whom they take a dislike.

They can harness their abundant energy constructively, tempering their self-confidence with shrewdness and their ambition with magnanimity towards others – provided they like them. If they do not, or if their feelings are neutral –

SEXUALITY

Marie Antoinette Queen of France Born 2 Novr. 7H 23 Mr. P.M. 1755.

ABOVE Mary Antoinette (1755–1793), born November 2, and her husband, Louis XVI (1755–1793), born August 23, were both guillotined.

Scorpio is the symbol of sex and Scorpians are passionate lovers, the most sensually energetic of all the signs. For them union with the beloved is a sacrament, an "outward and visible sign of an inward and spiritual grace." Their overriding urge in loving is to use their power to penetrate beyond themselves and to lose themselves sexually in their partners in an almost mystical ecstasy, thus discovering the meaning of that union which is greater than individuality and is a marriage of spirit as well as of flesh. They are thus capable of the greatest heights of passionate transport, but debauchery and perversion are always dangers, and Scorpians can become sadistic monsters of sensuality and eroticism. Their feelings are so intense that even when their love is of the highest and most idealistic kind, they are nevertheless frequently protagonists in tragic, even violent romances, "star-cross'd lovers" indeed.

unusual with them – they relate to fellow workers only as leaders and can be blunt to those they dislike to the point of cruelty. In fact they are not above expressing vindictiveness in deliberate cruelty. They are too demanding, too unforgiving of faults in others, perhaps because they are not unaware of the shortcomings within themselves, and extravagantly express their self-disgust in unreasonable resentment against their fellows. They do, however, make excellent friends, provided that their companions do nothing to impugn the honour of which Scorpians are very jealous. Part of the negative side of the Scorpian nature is a tendency to discard friends once they cease to be useful, but the decent native is aware of and fights this tendency.

They are fortunate in that their strong reasoning powers are tempered with imagination and intuition, and these gifts, together with critical perception and analytical capacity, can enable Scorpians to penetrate to profundities beyond the average. They have perhaps a better chance of becoming geniuses than the natives of any other sign. But charismatic "twice-born" characters such as they can sink into extremes of depravity if they take the wrong path, and the intensity of their natures exaggerates their harmful tendencies into vices far greater than the normal. Rebelliousness against all conventions, political extremism to the point where hatred of the Establishment makes them utterly unscrupulous terrorists, brooding resentment, aggressive and sadistic brutality, total arrogance, morbid jealousy, extreme volatility of temperament – these are some of their vices. At the other extreme is the procrastinator, the man or woman who is capable of so much that they do nothing and become indolent and self-indulgent, requiring extravagant praise and flattery from those whom they make their cronies.

FAMOUS SCORPIANS

Martin Luther (c1483–1546), born November 10. He possessed the Scorpio qualities of emotional energy, intensity, tenacity, conviction of his own rightness and spiritual fervour.

Theodore Roosevelt (1858–1919). The 26th President: immense willpower, tenacity and aggression – all Scorpian traits.

Marie Curie (1867–1934), born November 7, she was a typical Scorpian in the intensity and concentration she brought to her chemical research into radioactive substances and radium.

H.R.H. Prince Charles, Prince of Wales, November 14, 1948. In his public life he exhibits several Scorpio qualities – affability and courtesy in company, and passionate conviction about those matters (such as architecture) which he makes his concern.

Beings so gifted can find fulfillment in many employments. Their inner intensity can result in the ice-cold self-control and detachment of the surgeon, the concentration of the research scientist and the heroism of the soldier. Any profession in which analysis, investigation, research, dealing with practicalities and the solving of mysteries are relevant can appeal to them. So police and detective work, espionage and counter-espionage, the law, physics or psychology may attract them, and they can become masters of the written and spoken word. They may be most influential and persuasive orators and find fulfillment as diplomats or preachers and, if they make the Church their profession, their inner intensity can express itself in the spiritual fervour of the mystic of the thaumaturge.

They can become the kind of person to whom miracles become commonplace, spiritual healers, bearers of the stigmata and candidates for canonization when they have died. They make good psychical researchers, or even material for psychical research themselves.

Physically they tend to be of average height with strong, capable, thick-set, hirsute bodies, bow legs and a short neck. Their skulls are dome-shaped and their hair is coarse, thick and curly. Their faces are broad and square, with swarthy complexions, dark eyes and aquiline noses. They have strong constitutions, resistant to disease.

Scorpio governs the pelvis and reproductive and urinary systems and its subjects are said to be prone to ailments of the liver and kidneys, stones and gravel in the bladder or genitals, and other genital ills such as priapism. Abscesses, boils, carbuncles, fistulas, piles, ruptures and ulcers may also affect the Scorpian.

BELOW Scorpio, as depicted in a series of zodiacal signs in the interior of an Egyptian mummy-case of the 2nd century A.D.

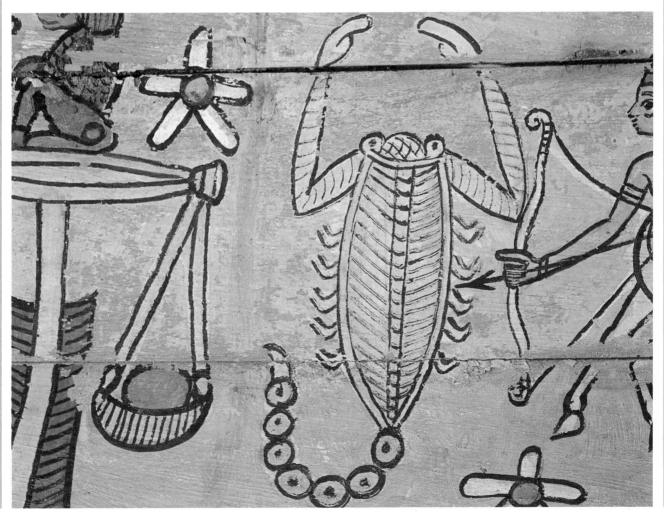

† SAGITTARIUS †

The good Sagittarian has a positive outlook on life, full of enterprise, energy, versatility, adventurousness and eagerness to extend his experience beyond the physically familiar. He enjoys travelling and exploration, the more so because his mind also is constantly open to new dimensions of thought. He is basically ambitious and optimistic and continues to be so even if his hopes are often dashed, and his strongly idealistic nature can also suffer many disappointments without

being affected. He is honourable, honest, trustworthy, truthful, generous and sincere, with a passion for justice. He balances loyalty with independence. Sagittarians are usually modest and often religious, with a strong sense of morality, though they tend to over-emphasize the ethical codes they follow and worship beliefs about God rather than God Himself. This means that, negatively, they regard rigid, unloving, intolerant adherence to ritual and conventional codes as more important than the truths they symbolize or embody. They sometimes pay lip service to religions and political parties in which they have ceased to believe because the outward forms satisfy them. Yet they may not hesitate to switch allegiance in politics or change their systems of belief if they see personal advantages to themselves in doing so.

BELOW Scorpio and Sagittarius painted on the inside of an Egyptian mummy-case of the 2nd century AD. The tradition of depicting the Archer as a centaur, half man, half beast, seems as old as the sign itself.

ABOVE Another illustration of Sagittarius, in an English Psalter of about 1170.

They have both profound and widely ranging minds, equipped with foresight and good judgment, and they can be witty conversationalists. They love to initiate new projects (they make excellent researchers) and have an urge to understand conceptions that are new to them. They think rapidly, are intuitive and often original, but are better at adapting than inventing and are at their best when working with colleagues of other types of character that complement their own. They are strong willed and good at organizing, a combination that gives them the ability to bring any project they undertake to a successful conclusion. Their generosity can be balanced by their extreme care in handling their resources. They are usually on the side of the underdog in society – they will fight without regard for their own advantage for any cause they believe to be just, and are prepared to be rebellious.

Sagittarians are ardent, sincere and straightforward in love, normally conventional and in control of their sexual natures. But if thwarted they may easily allow their failure to embitter their whole lives or they may revenge themselves upon the opposite sex by becoming cynically promiscuous. They are more apt than the average to make an uncongenial alliance. If their marriages are successful, they will be faithful spouses and indulgent parents, but their innate restlessness and constant desire to widen their experience will inspire them to use even the most satisfying ménage as a base from which to set out on their travels. They need to feel free and are often faced with the choice of allowing their careers to take over their lives at the expense of their love of wife and

RESTLESSNESS

ABOVE Sir Winston Leonard Spencer Churchill (1874–1965), born November 30. He exhibited the Sagittarian enterprise, energy, perseverance and will to succeed that helped bring victory to the Allied cause in 1945.

Professionally Sagittarians have a ruthless lust for leadership and this makes them unwilling to face monotonous hard work. Their search for job satisfaction may cause them to change careers a number of times, the more so because they are so restless. If these tendencies are carried to extremes they may become people who never settle down or remain in one type of work long enough to be financially secure. Yet if they do choose a satisfactory career their conscientious professionalism combined with the pleasant manners that are usually theirs, will bring them satisfaction in the long run.

ABOVE Ludwig van Beethoven (1770–1827), born December 16 or 17. He had the Sagittarian gift of superb musicality and its vice of violent temper.

family. A Sagittarian could well sympathize with the husband who addressed his "Clarissa" on leaving her to go to the wars, "I could not love thee half so well, lov'd I not honour more." Sagittarian women are the counterparts of their men. Even if they have no career to rival their love, they find it difficult to express affection and may run the risk of being thought frigid. In other personal relationships they are reliable, seldom betraying any trust given to them. They can, however, be impulsively angry and both male and female Sagittarians know how to be outspoken and exactly what expressions will hurt their adversaries most. On the other hand they are magnanimous in forgiving offences and are responsible when looking after the old people in the family.

Their gifts fit Sagittarians for a number of widely differing professions. They are natural teachers and philosophers with a talent for expounding the moral principles and laws which seem to explain the universe. This gift enables them to be successful churchmen on the one hand and scientists on the other. The law and politics also suit them, as does public service, social administration, public relations and advertising. Travel and exploration natually appeal to such restless souls and, if their opportunities are limited, they may find something of travel and change of scene in the armed forces or through working as a travelling salesman. Others may make

fine musicians and, in the days before automobiles, they were said to be successful at horse trading and all activities, including sporting ones, concerning horses. This has been translated in modern terms into an interest in cars and aircraft – and again with emphasis on the sporting side – racing, rallying, etc. They are said to make good sports coaches, but their tastes in this direction may lead them into imprudent gambling, though the gambling instinct can be sublimated by carrying it out professionally as a bookmaker.

The vices to which Sagittarians are prone are anger – they tend to flare up over trifles; impatience – they want to rush every new project through immediately and demand too much of colleagues who cannot work at the pace they require; and scorn of the inadequacies of others while expecting fulsome recognition of their own efforts. They may in one sense deserve recognition, because in completing a major project, they will sacrifice their own health and family relationships; in their family's eyes they may merit condemnation.

They can be exacting, domineering and inconsiderate in their workplace, and boastful, vulgar and extravagant in their private lives. Their restlessness, if excessive, can jeopardize more than their own stability. Some Sagittarians risk becoming playboys, wasting their lives away in frivolous pursuits. Others can develop a moralizing, religious fanaticism and, like Shakespeare's Malvolio, appear to be "sick of self-love," or else turn into hypocrites, their inner prudishness disguised by an outward appearance of joviality. Another side of the religiosity which is a danger in Sagittarians is superstition.

Physically those born under Sagittarius are said to possess strong, wiry, well-proportioned bodies of a little above average height. They have a dignified carriage and a handsome appearance. They are long-skulled with open, expressive oval faces, high foreheads and large front teeth in a narrow jaw. Their complexion is darkish – they suntan easily and attractively – and their hair is a light brown. They are also inclined to baldness. They are apt to be highly strung, a characteristic that can lead to nervous breakdowns in some.

Sagittarius governs the hips, thighs and sacral area; subjects suffer from ailments of the hips and thighs and are liable to sciatica and rheumatism. An alleged deficiency of silicon in their physiques can give them poor skin, nails and hair.

As they are often sportsmen indulging in dangerous pursuits, they are prone to the accidents that arise from these – the ancient astrologers mention falls from horses and hurts from them and other four-footed beasts. The taking of risks in other sports is a danger to the modern Sagittarian, and he is also liable to accidents with fire and heat.

LEFT Frank Sinatra, born December 12, 1915. Doing it his way, in true Sagittarian spirit.

BELOW Mark Twain (Samuel Langhorne Clemens) (1835–1910), born November 30. A Sagittarian in his love of travel, professionalism as a writer and successful marriage.

† CAPRICORN †

The Capricornian is one of the most stable and serious of the zodiacal types. These independent, rocklike characters have many sterling qualities, although admittedly some of these are as dull as they are worthy. This type is normally cautiously confident, strong willed and calm. Hardworking, unemotional, shrewd, practical, responsible, persevering – they are capable of persisting for as long as is necessary – they are reliable workers in almost any profession they undertake. But they are neither original nor creative and can only develop or organize what others invent or initiate. Within their limits, however, they are resourceful, determined managers, setting themselves and others high standards. Honest in their criticism of self, they respect discipline from above and demand it from those beneath them. In their slow, tough, stubborn, unyielding way they persist against boredom, frustration and hardship to reach their objectives long after more brilliant and volatile subjects have given up. In fact when practical business ability allied with the drive of ambition and lust for power and wealth are required in employees to make a project succeed, Capricornians are the men to hire. They plan carefully to fulfill their ambitions (which often include becoming wealthy), are economical without meanness and able to achieve great results with minimum effort and expense. Because of their organizing ability they are able to work on several projects simultaneously.

They love authority but may not be popular if they reach high rank, for, self-disciplined themselves, they expect their underlings to be equally so and to perform every task undertaken to the highest standard. They are, nevertheless, fair as well as demanding. Among their equals they are not always the most pleasant of work fellows either, for they are reserved and too conservative, valuing tradition more than innovation, however valuable the latter, and they are often humourless. There is also a tendency to pessimism, melancholy and even surliness which many Capricornians are unable to keep to themselves, especially if they fail personally or do not achieve

CAPRICIOUSNESS

ABOVE Edgar Allen Poe (1809–1849), poet and short-story writer, creator of the American Gothic tale. His deep depressions can be seen as Capricornian.

The swings in mood are not the only reason Capricornians deserve the adjective based on their name – capricious. They can be surprisingly and suddenly witty and subtle for the dull, prosaic creatures they seem to be, and they also have a tendency to ruin everything earned by their caution and shrewdness by unexpected and utterly irresponsible bouts of flippancy. In individuals in whom the characteristic is strong, the temptation to do this has to be resisted with iron self-control. Another unexpected quality in some Capricornians is an interest in the occult which persists in spite of their naturally sceptical turn of mind.

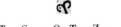

BELOW The more usual though more bizarre portrayal of Capricorn is to be seen in the roundel taken from an English Psalter, York, c1170.

ABOVE This naturalistic illustration of Capricorn from a mid-15th century French Calendar and Book of Hours is in marked contrast to the mythical creature with a goat's head and body and a fish's tail, usually knotted.

the corporate success which they had planned for their firms. They can spread gloom and tension in their circle which depresses everyone around them. In the extreme this trait can make them manic-depressive, ecstatic happiness alternating with the most wretched of misery for no reason that the subject of these emotions can name.

Their intellects are sometimes very subtle. They think profoundly though with little originality, have good memories and an insatiable yet methodical desire for knowledge. They are rational, logical and clear headed, have good concentration, delight in debate in which they can show off their clevernes by luring their adversaries into traps and confounding them with logic.

In their personal relationships they are often ill-at-ease, if not downright unhappy. They are self-centred, wary and suspicious of others, and in turn attract people who neither trust nor understand them. They prefer not to meddle with others nor to allow interference with themselves. Casual acquaintances they treat with diplomacy, tact and, above all,

ABOVE Elvis Aaron Presley (1935–1977), born January 8. "A strong attraction to music" is supposed to be a Capricornian characteristic, which understates the case somewhat for the King of Rock'n'Roll.

reticence. They make few good friends but are intensely loyal to those they do make, and they are bitter, revengeful enemies. They sometimes actively dislike the opposite sex and test the waters of affection gingerly before judging the temperature right for marriage. Once wedded, however, they are faithful, though inclined to jealousy. Family life, if well ordered as they like it to be, more than balances the goatlike inclination to lechery and inconstancy which some old authorities have ascribed to Capricorns.

Besides those already mentioned, faults to which the type is prone are over-conventionality, bigotry, selfishness, carelessness about personal appearance, avarice and miserliness, chronic complaining, incessant unnecessary worrying, and severity spilling over into cruelty.

Their occupations can include most professions that have to do with maths or money and they are strongly attracted to music. They can be economists, financiers, bankers, speculators, contractors, managers and also estate agents. They excel as bureaucrats, especially where projects demanding long-term planning and working are concerned, and their skill in debate and love of dialectic make them good politicians. They are excellent teachers, especially as principals of educational establishments where they have the authority

to manage and organize without too much intimacy with the staff members. If working with their hands, they can become practical scientists, engineers, farmers and builders. The wit and flippancy which is characteristic of certain Capricornians may make some turn to entertainment as a career.

Physically they have thin bodies and are below average height, with lean, narrow-chinned faces. The long skull, crowned with sparse black hair, sits on a scrawny neck, and moustache and beard are also thin. They are narrow chested and may be weak kneed, a handicap that gives them an ungainly bearing. In spite of their unprepossessing physique, Capricornians have a reasonably strong constitution. Many of the ailments of which they frequently complain – for they are inclined to hypochondria – are psychosomatic and due to their natural melancholia and depression.

Capricornus governs the knees, bones and skin, so its subjects may be liable to fractures and strains of the knees and other defects of the legs. Skin diseases from rashes and boils to leprosy (in countries where that disease is prevalent) are dangers, and digestive upsets may be caused by the Capricornian's tendency to worry or suppress emotions. Anaemia, Bright's disease, catarrh, deafness, rheumatism and rickets are also said to threaten the natives of this sign.

FAMOUS CAPRICORNS

Richard Nixon, born January 9, 1913. He possessed the Capricornian qualities of persistence, ambition for authority and attraction to a political career, and self-pity.

Louis Pasteur (1822–1895), born December 27. The French chemist and microbiologist, pioneer of vaccination, wrote, "will, work and success . . . fill human existence" – almost a Capricornian manifesto!

Sir Isaac Newton (1642–1727), born December 25. He was typically Capricornian in his mathematical genius and his secret interest in the occult (alchemy).

† AQUARIUS †

Aquarians basically possess strong and attractive personalities. They fall into two principal types: one shy, sensitive, gentle and patient; the other exuberant, lively and exhibitionist, sometimes hiding the considerable depths of their character under a cloak of frivolity. Both types are strong willed and forceful in their different ways and have strong convictions, though as they seek truth above all things, they are usually honest enough to change their opinions, however firmly held,

if evidence comes to light which persuades them that they have been mistaken. They have a breadth of vision that brings diverse factors into a whole, and can see both sides of an argument without shilly-shallying as to which side they take. Consequently they are unprejudiced and tolerant of other points of view. This is because they can see the validity of the arguments, even if they do not accept them themselves. They obey the Quaker exhortation to "Be open to truth, from whatever source it comes," and are prepared to learn from everyone.

Both types are humane, frank, serious minded, genial, refined, sometimes aetherial, and idealistic, though this last quality is tempered with a sensible practicality. They are quick, active and persevering without being self-assertive, and express themselves with reason, moderation and, sometimes, a dry humour.

BELOW Aquarius is usually represented, as here, as a man pouring out water. The picture on the left shows the two-headed god, Janus, looking back to the past year and forward to the new.

INDEPENDENCE

ABOVE Charles Robert Darwin (1809–1882), born February 12. Known mainly for his *Origin of Species,* he was Aquarian in the significance and radicalism of his scientific research, in his retiring nature, and in his loyalty to family and friends.

Aquarians are independent, respecting neither authority nor convention unless they are satisfied that there are sound and convincing reasons for them. They see through pretentiousness and pomp and will energetically support causes, sometimes extreme, which oppose the Establishment. But they are both too tolerant and too intelligent to become nihilistic revolutionaries or terrorists, for all that they are original and progressive thinkers. They are fonder of innovation and reforms than they are of conservation of things as they are.

They are nearly always intelligent, concise, clear and logical. Many are strongly imaginative and physically intuitive, so that the Age of Aquarius, which is about to begin, is much anticipated by psychic circles as an age in which mankind will experience a great spiritual awakening. The Aquarian philosophical and spiritual bent may be dangerous in that it can drive the subjects into an ivory-tower existence where they meditate on abstractions that bear little relevance to life. On the other hand it can help the many who have scientific leanings to combine these with the Aquarian yearning for the universal recognition of the brotherhood of man, and to embark on scientific research to fulfill their philanthropic ideals of benefiting mankind. When some cause or work of this nature inspires them, they are capable of such devotion to it that they may drive themselves to the point of exhaustion and even of injuring their health.

Both types need to retire from the world at times and to become temporary loners. They appreciate opportunities for meditation or, if they are religious, of retreats. Even in com-

ABOVE Abraham Lincoln (1809–1865), born February 12. The 16th President of the United States showed in his public career the humaneness, sensitivity and far-sightedness of the Aquarian.

pany they are fiercely independent, refusing to follow the crowd. They dislike interference by others, however helpfully intended, and will accept it only on their own terms. Normally they have good taste in drama, music and art, and are often gifted in the arts, especially drama.

In spite of the often intensely magnetic, forthcoming and open personality of the more extrovert kind of Aquarian, and of their desire to help humanity, neither type makes friends easily. They sometimes appear to condescend to others and take little trouble to cultivate the acquaintance of people who do not particularly appeal to them. They do not give themselves easily – perhaps their judgment of human nature is too good for that – and are sometimes accounted cold. But once they decide that someone is worthy of their friendship or love, they can exert an almost hypnotic and irresistible mental attraction on them and will themselves become tenacious

FAMOUS AQUARIANS

Franklin Delano Roosevelt (1882–1945), born January 30. The 32nd President of the United States, "one of the most loved and most hated men in U.S. history."

Thomas Alva Edison (1847–1931), born February 11. He developed the telephone, invented the phonograph and took out over a thousand patents in electrical inventions.

Vanessa Redgrave, born January 30, 1937. The English actress displays Aquarian characteristics in her anti-establishment politics as well as her wonderful acting abilities.

ABOVE Aquarius is depicted in a 16th-century Turkish treatise on astrology as drawing water from a well. Eastern and western artistic conventions frequently differ in presentation even when dealing with similar ideas or symbols.

friends or lovers, ready to sacrifice everything for their partners and be faithful to them for life. However, they are sometimes disappointed emotionally because their own high personal ideals cause them to demand more of others than is reasonable. And if they are deceived their anger is terrible. If disillusioned, they do not forgive.

Aquarians work best in group projects, provided that they are recognized as having a leading part in them. They have a feeling of unity with nature and a desire for knowledge and truth that makes them admirable scientists, especially astronomers and natural historians. They may excel in photography, radiography, electronics – anything connected with the electrical and radio industries – aviation and everything technical. On the arts and humanities side their progressive tendencies can be expressed in writing, especially poetry, and broadcasting, or as social workers and teachers. Some have gifts as entertainers and make good character actors (having an ability to mimic) and musicians. The more psychic among them possess healing gifts, especially in curing the mentally sick.

Among the faults to which they are liable are fanatical eccentricity, wayward egotism, excessive detachment and an inclination to retreat from life and society, and a tendency to be extremely dogmatic in their opinions. Circumstances – for example, continuous opposition to a cause they hold dear – may cause the atrophy of the openness of mind that is one of the Aquarian's most attractive traits. They may express a lack of integrity in broken promises, secretiveness and cunning. Simmering anger and resentment, rudeness or, worse, a tense, threatening silence which may suddenly burst out in eruptions of extreme temper, these are all part of the negative side of the Aquarian. This can also reveal itself in a sustained hatred for enemies that is capable of enlarging itself into a misanthropy towards the whole of mankind.

Physically Aquarians are said to be of below average height, stocky and inclined to stoutness. Their constitutions are poor. They have long skulls and faces and are usually good looking – the men are sometimes handsome in an almost feminine way – with ruddy complexions and light flaxen or sandy hair in youth which darkens as they grow older. They have blue or hazel eyes.

As Aquarius is said to govern the legs from knees to ankles and the circulation of the blood, its natives are susceptible to ailments particularly in the legs and ankles, such as cramps, and are also liable to spasmodic and nervous complaints, as well as wind, catarrh, diarrhea, dropsy, goitre and delirium tremens – so that the avoidance of alcohol is important for those Aquarians who have a taste for it.

✝ PISCES ✝

Pisces is one of the less flamboyant signs and its natives are more ordinary than those of, for example, Leo, Scorpio and Aquarius. Pisceans possess a gentle, patient, malleable nature. They have many generous qualities and are friendly, good natured, kind and compassionate, sensitive to the feelings of those around them, and respond with the utmost sympathy and tact to any suffering they encounter. They are deservedly popular with all kinds of people, partly because their easy-going, affectionate, submissive natures offer no threat or challenge to stronger and more exuberant characters. They accept the people around them and the circumstances in which they find themselves rather than trying to adapt them to suit themselves, and they patiently wait for problems to sort themselves out rather than take the initiative in solving them. They are more readily concerned with the problems of others than with their own.

RIGHT The 16th-century Turkish illustration depicts Pisces as transportation for (presumably) the astrologer.

BELOW Pisces is commonly represented as two fishes swimming in opposite directions, their mouths joined by a line. The latter owes its existence to a string of stars which joins the groups that form the fishes.

Their natures tend to be too other-worldly for the practical purposes of living in this world as it is. They exist emotionally rather than rationally, instinctively more than intellectually. Their willpower, ambition – they long to be recognized as greatly creative – and reasoning are all limited and, however anxious they are to fulfil themselves, their concentration is weak; they lack decisiveness and they are easily diverted from their purposes. They are apt to live a shiftless sort of life, searching for some career in which they can really find

Elizabeth Taylor, born 27 February, 1932. A Piscean in her artistic ability, perhaps also in her previous alcoholic addiction; but no-one could argue for any Piscean submissiveness in her character, judging from the public persona at least (always a potentially misleading exercise).

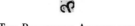
themselves, but being easily discouraged they become despondent, feeling unappreciated and moving on to something or someone else. They also dislike discipline and confinement within routine – the nine to five life is not for them – and confinement by codes of behaviour. Any rebellion they make against convention is personal, however, as they do not have the energy to battle against the Establishment.

They are never egotistical in their personal relationships and give more than they ask from their friends. They are sexually delicate, in the extreme almost asexual, and most Pisceans would want a relationship in which the partner's mind and spirit rather than the body resonated with their own. Unfortunately they can be easily misled by a lover who courts them delicately and in marriage makes them unhappy by a coarser sexuality than they expected. They are nevertheless intensely loyal and home-loving and will remain faithful – though their dreamy and impractical natures do not fit them to keep a tidy and well-run house.

In their employment they are better working either by themselves or in subordinate positions. Their talents are individual – in a commercial business or similar undertaking they would be afraid to manage more than a small department, worrying always that they would fail in a crisis. They can make fair secretaries and bookkeepers. Their sympathy equips them for work in charities catering for the needy, as nurses looking after the sick and as veterinary surgeons caring for animals. As librarians or astronomers they can satisfy their mental wanderlust, and their fondness for "faraway places with strange-sounding names" may turn them into sailors or travellers. Many architects and lawyers are Pisceans, and when the creative abilities are combined with gifts of imitation and the ability to enter into the feelings of others, Pisceans find their fulfillment on the stage. Their psychic and spiritual qualities can lead them to careers in the Church or as mediums and mystics. They may find an outlet for their creativity as caterers, and are said to make good detectives because they

CREATIVITY

Pisceans tend to withdraw into a dreamworld where their qualities can bring them mental satisfaction and sometimes, but by no means inevitably, fame and financial reward – for they are gifted artistically. They are also versatile and intuitive, have quick understanding, observe and listen well, and are receptive to new ideas and atmospheres. All these factors can combine to produce remarkable creativity in literature, music and art. They may count

among their gifts mediumistic qualities which can give them a feeling that their best work comes from outside themselves, "Whispered beyond the misted curtains, screening this world from that." Even when they cannot express themselves creatively they have a greater than average instinct for, and love of, beauty in art and nature, a catlike appreciation of luxury and pleasure, and a yearning for new sensations and travel to remote, exotic places.

LEFT George Frederick Handel (1685–1759), born February 23. The Anglo-German composer is an excellent example of the Piscean qualities that can produce remarkable creativity in music.

can imagine themselves in the place of criminals and understand how their minds would work. In technical occupations they are well employed in dealing with anesthetics, fluids, gases and plastics. Because of their lively versatility and inability to concentrate over-much on any one project, Pisceans often simultaneously follow more than one occupation.

Their faults are exasperating rather than vicious. They can be over-subtle, over-sensitive and over-emotional. In business they can be unreliable, idle, careless, impractical and ineffective. Their friends may find their diffidence and sense of their own unimportance irritating and may eventually want to shake off acquaintances who not only lack initiative but are peevish and extravagantly temperamental in their dependence on them. Other faults of which the negative Piscean is accused are fickleness, gossiping, indiscretion, effeminacy and gullibility. They may not be able to avoid being sickly, but their fretting hypochondria can wear out a saint's patience. They can be intellectually dishonest and also actually fraudulent, deceitful and hypocritical. They are often indecisive in important matters yet will uphold absurdities with the obstinacy of the weak. When they feel themselves rejected, lonely or failures, or simply through feeble self-indulgence, they will find refuge in drugs or the bottle.

Pisceans are said to be slightly below average height, with poor physiques and weak constitutions. Their bodies are fleshy, squat-limbed and stooping, their faces large and their complexions pale. Their hair and eyes are usually brown and the latter are often protruding and hooded.

Pisces governs the feet, liver and lymphatics, and its subjects can be threatened by anemia, boils, ulcers and other skin diseases, especially inflammation of the eyelids, gout, inflammation, heavy periods and foot disorders and lameness.

In addition to the individual characteristics listed above, the signs of the zodiac are classified in three other ways. Each is either positive (masculine) or negative (feminine); each is assigned one of the four elements of fire, air, earth and water (known as the triplicities because there are three signs to each element); and each is either cardinal, fixed or mutable (the quadruplicities because there are four signs to each division). Positive signs are spontaneous and self-expressive, negative signs withdrawn and passive. Fire is lively and aggressive; earth matter-of-fact and controlled; air lively in mind and fluent in expression; water sensitive and intuitive. The qualities of cardinal, fixed and mutable are, respectively, initiative, steadfastness and changeableness/adaptability. The table lists these characteristics.

TABLE 8
CHARACTERISTICS OF THE SIGNS

Sign		Quality	Triplicity	Quadruplicity	Ruler
Aries	♈	Positive	Fire	Cardinal	Mars
Taurus	♉	Negative	Earth	Fixed	Venus
Gemini	♊	Positive	Air	Mutable	Mercury
Cancer	♋	Negative	Water	Cardinal	Moon
Leo	♌	Positive	Fire	Fixed	Sun
Virgo	♍	Negative	Earth	Mutable	Mercury
Libra	♎	Positive	Air	Cardinal	Venus
Scorpio	♏	Negative	Water	Fixed	Mars
Sagittarius	♐	Positive	Fire	Mutable	Jupiter
Capricorn	♑	Negative	Earth	Cardinal	Saturn
Aquarius	♒	Positive	Air	Fixed	*Uranus
Pisces	♓	Negative	Water	Mutable	Jupiter

*Formerly Saturn.

CHAPTER THREE

THE PLANETS AND CHARACTERISTICS OF THE HOUSES

There were seven planets (Greek *planetae* meaning "wanderers," because they could be seen to move against the background of the fixed constellations) known to the ancients, apart from the Earth itself. These were the Sun and Moon, Mercury, Venus, Mars, Jupiter and Saturn. They conveniently suited the seven days of the week which were named after them, or deities which were the equivalent of the classical gods and goddesses in Scandinavian mythology. So we have Sun-day, Mo(o)nday, Tyr's or Tiw's-day (Tiw was Mars), Woden'sday (Woden was Mercury), Thor'sday (Thor and Jupiter were both gods of thunder), Frigg or Frea'sday (Frea was the Scandinavian Venus) and Satur(n's)day. The neatness of the fit of the seven planets into the week, which was a fourth of the moon's cycle, and their association with the prime number 7, significant in numerology, added to the authority of astrology – which was somewhat spoiled when other planets were discovered that upset the scheme.

Astrologers retort by claiming that the seven planets that can be seen with the naked eye are close enough to have an effect on human character. Those discovered after the invention of the telescope are so distant that any influence they exert will be over decades – even generations and centuries (Pluto takes 248 years to circle the sun and the zodiac once) – and is therefore miniscule for the individual compared with the seven formerly recognized.

An adequate horoscope can certainly be erected using only the seven original planets, but for completeness' sake the characteristics of Uranus (discovered 1781), Neptune (calculated 1845, observed 1846) and Pluto (discovered 1930) are here included.

Each planet is given a special relationship with one or two zodiacal signs and houses. It was observed by astrologers that the position of a planet in a chart suggested certain characteristics similar to those traditionally associated with the gods and goddesses named.

The traits attached to each planet in the following summaries describe the unadulterated qualities which each is said to possess. In practice they are always modified by the positions of other planets and signs of the zodiac – as will be seen when we study aspects and other relationships in the horoscope – and are interpreted initially as showing no more than tendencies in the subject's character.

SUN

The Sun is the head of the solar system and has more obvious influence on life on Earth than any other heavenly body. As the "father" of its family of planets, it represents universal fatherhood and therefore the male principle. In Christian thought, during the ages when astrology was universally accepted as a recognized science, the Sun's usually beneficent power and vitality were symbolic of the fatherhood of God and his use of the creative power of nature to affect almost everything on Earth, including human beings.

The Sun exerts the most powerful astrological influence of any heavenly body on the personality and some astrologers claim that the knowledge of an individual's Sun sign alone (that sign of the zodiac in which the Sun is to be found at the native's birth) can give a picture of his character that will be 80 percent or more accurate.

For both sexes the Sun represents self-integration, wholeness of being, authority, energy, vitality, forcefulness and a positive outlook. For a man it governs his generative and creative power in the widest sense of the words, including his position as head of his household and the career he will follow. To a woman it represents the men in her life, but increasingly, as women progress in pursuing professions of their own, she may look for interpretations of the Sun's influence in her horoscope along the same lines as men.

The native with the Sun prominent in his chart may be a natural leader with a strong intellect, qualities which in combination should bring him success. But just as too much Sun is at best unpleasant and at worst disastrous, so an excess of ability to command may lead to arrogance, bombast and flamboyance, and the intellectual strength spills over into intolerance. Because the human who displays these negative qualities

ABOVE The Sun: from a 1531 series of woodcuts by Hans Sebold Beham illustrating the planets. The Sun's subjects are depicted as wealthy, and gaudy.

BELOW Worship of the Sun-Disc, in the Gandhara (modern Pakistan) style of sculpture, with Greek and Roman influence, 1st to 2nd centuries AD.

believes he is superior in leadership and intelligence, he is liable to be more fallible through rashness in a crisis than someone who has a more moderate view of his own abilities.

The heart conveys the elements of life to the whole body, and in like manner the Sun pulsates heat and light to the entire solar system. So, physiologically, the Sun affects the whole physical body, energizing it through the heart. In particular the Sun governs the thymus gland, which regulates the body's rate of growth, just as the Sun controls the growth of crops and living creatures.

The Sun represents spiritual energy, and not only in the individual. The mental equipment of mankind consists of the conscious mind, and the many-layered subconscious mind. Also, according to Jung, there is the collective unconscious, or universal subconscious. Jung believed that the collective subconscious contains psychic material passed down from generation to generation of humans and that we all share in it. It expresses itself in archetypes, dreams and fears which occasionally come to us from a deeper level than our individual subconsciousness. So just as the Earth turns each part of its area in turn toward the Sun, so that its light and heat touch most of the planet every 24 hours, so the spiritual energy of the astrological Sun affects the collective consciousness of mankind.

The symbol of the Sun is a dot within a circle. The dot represents the nucleus of the individual, the circle his completeness. The circle also expresses divine spirit and eternity or everlastingness, and much more can be read into the symbolism by those who care to reflect on it.

The Sun rules in Leo, its house is the fifth, its day Sunday, its best hours the first, eighth, fifteenth and twenty-second.

MOON

The Moon, though regarded by the ancient Babylonians as male, is the planet of predominantly feminine qualities, both positive and negative. It is also the ruler of the soul and the individual's "desire nature." The good qualities she controls

ABOVE A partial eclipse of the Sun, July 20 1982. What a terrifying sight this must have been before Man began to unlock the secrets of the physical universe.

BELOW The Sun, as illustrated in a 14th-century Italian treatise on astrology.

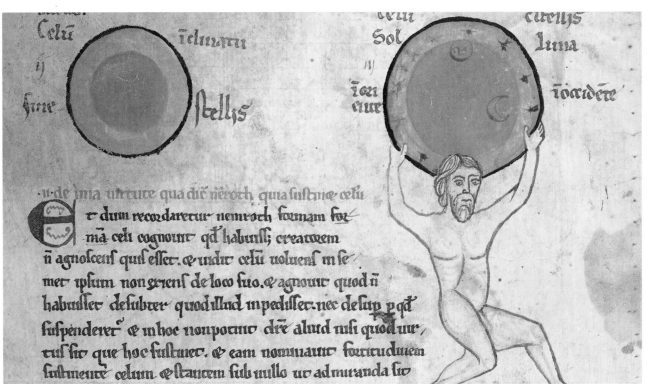

ABOVE Carl Gustav Jung (1875–1967) taught that there existed a collective subconsciousness of mankind. Astrology believes that this may be energized by the spiritual influence of the Sun.

RIGHT Symbolic representation of occupations connected with water with which the Moon is assocated. Above is Diana, the Moon goddess, holding a crescent, the planet's symbol. Her chariot wheel bears the sign of Cancer.

are sure intuition, delicacy of feeling, aesthetic receptivity and affection – especially within the family, between siblings, or for children by parents – for lunar love is nonsexual, chaste and often spiritual. Spiritual also is the intelligence the Moon bestows on its natives, since they use their experience of life to develop the reverential side of their characters and the sensitivity of their inner natures. Such characters will inevitably be introspective which is no bad quality provided that it is controlled. The lunar woman may well be an ardent feminist, proud of her sex and of the qualities belonging to it, yet deeply maternal and protective of her family. Both she and her male counterpart may have a strong sense of loyalty and patriotism.

Not such good qualities of the lunar character are its moodiness, restlessness – often expressed in arbitrary changes of mind and outlook – impressionability, impulsiveness, and tendency to join with the crowd in doing what everyone else is doing, following the fashion of the moment. The character's placidity can easily degenerate into passivity and timidity, or

become boring, as the aesthetic sensitivity may deteriorate into fantasy and dreaminess. There is also a risk that a Moon-man may develop a mother-complex.

The Moon is associated with water and its influence on the tides causes it to symbolize change and motion, though in a rhythmic rather than an anarchic fashion. Rhythm, both in the ebb and flow of the sea and the Moon's waxing and waning, is a symbol of pregnancy, while the conjunction of the Sun and new Moon signifies copulation. More generally, the Moon's cycle portrays the physical change of life, growth from birth to maturity followed by a gradual decay back into nothingness.

The planet also indicates astrologically the struggle, to be found in all human beings, between the flesh and the spirit, for the Moon is pulled in one direction by the Sun, symbolizing spirit, and in another by the Earth, portraying matter. This does not mean that the lunar character necessarily exhibits inconsistency to those who know him, and the appearance or not of the inner struggle depends largely on the position of the Moon in relation to other planets. A conjunction of Moon and Sun, for example, presents a subject who is exactly what he appears to be; but if Sun and Moon are opposed, the

individual will see himself as possessing one kind of character while observers may see a quite different and even opposite type. If the Moon is in aspect (see page 23 for full explanation) with just one other planet, consistent conduct of one kind or another will appear, but if there are aspects between the Moon and many planets the result is a person who fits his or her behaviour to the company. If the Moon's influence is very prominent in a subject's horoscope it may be expressed in a way that is uncharacteristic of the delicacy, sensitivity and spirituality generally associated with the planet, going beyond these and causing him to call attention to himself in his profession, whatever that may be. Thus he may be an amusing entertainer, not afraid of exhibitionism if it raises a laugh, or a politician whose witty speeches, artfully worked at, could earn him advancement, especially if backed by the more solid lunar qualities.

Physiologically the Moon governs the autonomic system, with its numerous nervous reflexes and the automatic physical responses we develop from our birth. It also rules the stomach, womb, ovaries, breasts and pancreas. A faulty pancreas can give rise to emotional instability and, rightly or wrongly, the association of extreme weakness of this kind with the phases of the Moon has given rise to the word "lunatic" to describe

madness. The Moon also influences body fluids, the circulation of the blood and the digestive and lymphatic systems that nourish, protect and lubricate. In addition to its effect on human physiology, the Moon is supposed especially to influence plant growth.

Psychically the Moon represents the right-hand hemisphere of the brain, the seat of intuition. As the Sun deals with the universal subconsciousness, so the Moon is the planet of the individual subliminal mind and its psychological characteristics. It links present and past, with the result that lunar personalities yearn nostalgically for times that are gone. If, however, they are balanced in outlook, they will use their memories and past experience as an inspiration for future action. The Moon, cyclic and rhythmic in its own behaviour, forms habit patterns in its subjects which result from the ebb and flow of sensation in them and their emotional responses to these.

The Moon's symbol is a crescent which, as an incomplete circle, represents the mind, the visible crescent symbolizing the conscious mind, the invisible remainder of the circle the subconscious. It rules in Cancer, the night-time house, appropriately a water sign; its house is the fourth, its day Monday, its best hours the second, ninth, sixteenth and twenty-fourth.

BELOW The heavenly body with which we are on the most intimate terms: an Apollo 12 photograph of the lunar surface featuring the crater Erastosthenes, 38 miles in diameter.

ABOVE As this extraordinary 17th-century French illustration shows, the effect of the Moon upon women was seen as pretty drastic. Heaven knows what was supposed to happen at the full moon.

ABOVE The rhythm of the Moon's waxing and waning is symbolic of pregnancy.

MERCURY

Because it is closest to its parent Sun and the smallest in the solar system, Mercury is regarded as the planet of childhood and youth. It has the greatest lineal speed and shortest sidereal period and these give it a sprightliness in comparison with the other planets that both supports the idea of youth and explains why, in mythology, it was regarded as the nimble messenger of the gods who had wings on his feet that whisked him through the skies.

To be mercurial is to possess an impetuous intuition, to sparkle with ready wit and to be agile, volatile, changeable and restless. The Mercurian is liable to have a good memory and to be intelligent, even brilliant, one of those lucky people who can pass examinations without ever seeming to do a stroke of work or needing to do one. But although he is strongly intellectual, greedy for knowledge and capable of great learning, his scholarship is likely to be wide, not profound, for he lacks application and prefers to change to learning a new skill or science rather than be bored by the effort needed to deepen what he already knows. He is strongly rational and objective, remains uncommitted in doubtful matters, and will sit charmingly and innocuously on any fence he can find.

If he becomes an educationalist, he will be a good one, for he enjoys teaching and is able to communicate. His enthusiasm will also fire his pupils, though they may sometimes be shaken by his sudden outbursts of temper, and he will not suffer fools gladly. That ability to communicate allied with his gifts of self-expression in speech and writing can also gain him a reputation in advertising or the media, where he

A Roman face urn from the late 2nd century AD, dedicated to Mercury.

could become a television personality or journalist. His eloquence makes him an expressive spokesman for the rights of others, so that he may find his niche in local or national government, or the organization of a charity.

He can turn his hand to many different kinds of career, and indeed may fail, comparatively, in the end, because his versatility will lead him to become a dilettante, a "jack of all trades and master of none." He may have considerable artistic ability, but his execution, though brilliant, will tend to superficiality and lack of seriousness. In technical pursuits he has inventiveness and skill in engineering and carpentry and may well become an expert in computerized communications systems. He loves to travel, especially where few have gone before, and is a trailblazer for others to follow. He can make a good doctor but will be a better general practitioner, than

BELOW Art, mathematics (including astrology), music – activities associated with Mercury – are shown beneath his chariot. Its wheels represent his "houses", Gemini and Virgo.

ABOVE 15th-century Italian illustration of workers in the fields under the influence of Mercury, accompanied by Gemini and Virgo. He holds a caduceus in his left hand.

specialist, for he will want variety in his work rather than depth. His personal relationships may bring unhappiness to others rather than to himself as his is a character which is comparatively unaffected in such matters. He may impress those who meet him with his air of innocent charm, which is often deceptive. In friendship and love his head rules his heart, and he is capricious, cold, selfish and calculating underneath the charm.

If he is law-abiding he may still have unpleasant characteristics – glibness, shallowness, cunning, artfulness, subtlety – a thoroughly slippery character. Even without these vices he may be frivolous, rashly impetuous and liable to make wrong decisions rather than acknowledge ignorance or lack of experience. He will also be prepared to cover up his shortcomings by lying and placing the blame on other people. It must not be forgotten that Mercury is the planet of childhood with its virtues of innocence and charm, and vice of lying to keep out of trouble, and some Mercurians never grow up. The planet is also the patron planet of thieves, and the felonious Mercurian will be a plausible rogue, an expert in the criminal world of confidence trickery (where his charm will bewitch his victims), fraud and insider dealing.

One side of Mercury is always exposed to the Sun, the other always turned away. These two sides correspond to the conscious and subconscious areas of the mind. Physically Mercury governs the brain as the seat of reason, logic, consciousness and the will, and as the interpreter of sensations and the unconscious; the central nervous system; and the thyroid, which controls, among other things, some specifically Mercurian qualities such as movement, volatility, nervous reaction, physical and mental growth, and critical functional changes during life.

Gemini and Virgo are the zodiacal signs ruled by Mercury, its houses are the third and sixth, its day is Wednesday and its hours the fourth, eleventh and eighteenth. Its symbol is a half-circle, the horns pointing upward, over a circle under-neath which is a cross. The half-circle is interpreted as representing human mind and spirit, the whole as completeness and the divine spirit, and the cross as matter. Alternatively, the symbol is said to be a conventional representation of the caduceus, the staff carried by Mercury as messenger of the gods and today used as an emblem by the medical profession. It consists of a rod with displayed wings at its upper end and two serpents intertwined around it.

VENUS

Venus, the only female planet, has an undeserved bad name through being associated, incorrectly, with unbridled sexual desire. It is only occasionally (see below) that her influence is exerted in this direction, and she is traditionally considered a good and beneficent planet. Venus was originally a goddess of spring and as such had a good deal to do with fertility and new life, hence with the sexual, procreative side of love, but

BELOW A contour map of the surface of the real Venus, shown on a Mercator projection. The white-centred red contour is a mountain higher than Everest. 35,400ft above what the scientists call "sea level."

BELOW A 15th-century representation of Venus and the fountain of eternal youth.

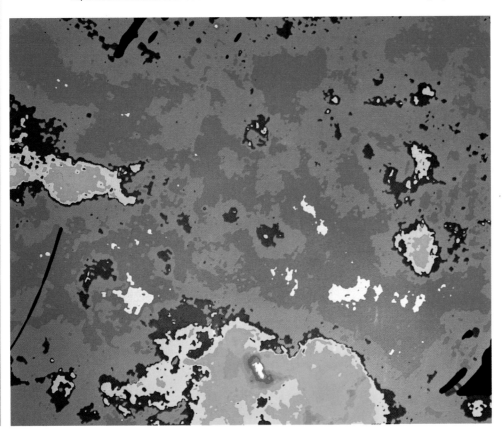

her care was much more exercised for close personal rela-
tionships of every kind – the deep affection of friends and the
pleasure they find in each other, the sacramental joy of the
sexes in their mutual desire, rather than lust, the outgoing
love of parents, especially mothers, for their children. Peace
and harmony are what Venus wishes for those whom she
brings together in friendship and love.

The Venusian is also alive to harmony of every kind, in
music and all the arts and in everything that has to do with
the outward appearance of people and objects. He admires
physical attractiveness in men and women, especially if their
beauty is combined with grace, elegance and fastidiousness.
All his senses are alert to pleasure. He enjoys loveliness of
every kind. His ear delights in listening to music, in which
he will be knowledgeable even if lacking in the ability to play
himself. He is a gourmet. He has a nose for delicacy in wine
or perfume, for such daintiness of scent is a mark of the
elegance he admires. He also likes to enjoy his body and feel
at home in it, so that he is likely to be a graceful dancer and,
if athletic, a stylish performer in his chosen sport. He will be
a sensitive lover. In a weak Venusian character sensuousness
may develop into voluptuousness and even a moderate subject will always prefer the experience of the senses to a
rationalized judgment.

In addition to his strongly creative, artistic and aesthetic
traits, the Venusian has a sunny, optimistic, witty disposition,
with an outgoing warmth and sympathy that longs both to give
and receive affection and appreciation. Both sexes are tactful,
value cooperation and unity of purpose with their partners,
and are contented with and single-mindedly faithful to each
other when there is a likelihood that these aims can be
achieved. Perhaps because of the satisfaction of having a
secure home-base, Venusians are good at work, especially in
business, in which they have the ability both to make and
take lucky chances and earn good money. Their admiration
for harmony, and elegance makes them haters of discord and
violence. In short, of evil generally, and they rule their lives
by high ideals which they set for themselves.

Because Venus represents the feminine qualities of which a
portion is necessary for a balanced character in both sexes,
the male Venusian may be (willingly!) under the thumb of the

RIGHT The Venus de Milo, mid-2nd century BC. arguably the most beautifully
proportioned female nude statue of all time, now in the Louvre, Paris.

ABOVE LEFT Venus is driven in her chariot by her blindfold son, Cupid. Her chariot wheels show Taurus and Libra as her "houses."

ABOVE RIGHT Aphrodite (Venus) and Pan playing knucklebones, a drawing incised with metal points inside the cover of a Grecian mirror, c350 BC.

women in his life or be feminine in character himself. As the positive qualities are some of the most attractive mankind can possess, so the negative are among the more unpleasant. The male subject may be an effeminate and sycophantic, flattering, fawning weakling of a man and the female a yielding, passive, timorous wallflower of a woman. Both are likely to be dull and despised and to try to compensate for the loneliness that comes to them from boring their acquaintances by sordid and promiscuous love affairs. These unpleasing characteristics are the more possible when Venus is affected by some other planets and certain zodiacal signs. If she is in conjunction with the Sun she increases the chance of effeminacy in her male subjects. In Gemini she strengthens the tendency to fickleness and promiscuity. In Scorpio she inspires an intensely passionate sexual drive which may be difficult to control. When Venus is square to Saturn her subjects will have to guard against selfishness. When she is in conjunction with Saturn or Mercury, husbands not on good terms with their Venus wives because of the latters' attempts to dominate them should beware of their cooking, remembering that the traditional murder weapon of women is poison.

Venus governs the parathyroid glands in the human body. These control the calcium content in the organism and build the framework of the skeleton, thus satisfying the principle of unity which is characteristic of the planet. The lumbar region is also under Venus' sway. Her subjects are at risk of gastric troubles through their fondness for spicy foods, and genital diseases because of their sexual natures.

Venus' symbol is the archetypal female sign for the feminine gender, consisting of a circle above a cross. As in symbols already mentioned the circle represents completeness and divine spirit, and the cross matter. The planet is associated with Taurus and Libra. She rules in the second and seventh houses. Her day is Friday and her hours are the seventh, thirteenth and nineteenth.

MARS

Mars can be epitomized by the fourth of Shakespeare's famous seven ages of man (*As You Like It*, II. vii).

Then a soldier,
Full of strange oaths, and bearded like the pard,
Jealous in honour, sudden and quick in quarrel,
Seeking the bubble reputation
Even in the cannon's mouth.

RIGHT A classical statue of Mars, representing the warrior image usually associated with him.

ABOVE The fully armed and armoured Mars in his chariot, its wheels bearing the symbols of his "houses," Aries and Scorpio.

BELOW Armed conflict, rapine, pillage and fire are seen underneath the chariot of Mars drawn by the dogs of war.

Traditionally a bad or malefic planet, Mars represents the masculine principle with its virtues and vices, especially men in their capacities as husbands and fathers. In feminine horoscopes it portrays male influence, especially that of the partner. The Martian character is enterprising, thorough, energetic, self-assertive, and enjoys hard work for the pleasure of feeling his body and mind respond to a challenge. He is a natural leader and can be a versatile pioneer, taking the initiative for changes, though usually only if the way is indicated by others, for he lacks the imagination to attempt things outside his experience and is happier in ways familiar to him. He can be taken at his face value, for he does not have the subtlety or patience to prevaricate and will sometimes make a virtue of a rough manner, brusque outspokenness and lack of refinement. There is little depth to him and he has no artistic leanings unless they can be expressed in, say, wrought iron, fashioned by the energy and physical strength of a smith.

He is usually a born soldier and is likely to be one of those characters who look back with nostalgia to the comradeship of war and claims never to have tasted life so fully as when in the heat of battle. He is without fear – largely because of his lack of imagination – cheerful, especially under stress, bold and tireless, driving himself to the limit, but as a leader in war needs the balance of more cautious officers on his staff, for he can be impatiently hasty, impulsive and excitable. He is easily angered by opposition but as effortlessly mollified, for he has that in him which will not take unnecessary risks, and can recognize good advice for what it is. In

civil matters he can be dignified, in public events show a sense of occasion, and if in high position display an imperial nobility that is impressive.

Another of his features is tenacity. If a scholar he will pursue his researches with a Teutonic thoroughness, if in a profession based on conviction, such as politics or the Church, he will cling to his principles in the face of ostracism or martyrdom.

An unadulterated Martian character would be so macho as to be appalling, for it would be violently aggressive, at best wantonly mischievous, at worst cruelly malevolent. Boisterous when sober, ruffianly when drunk, the subjects of the "rogue planet" are extravagant in their dress and accoutrements, rapacious vandals who love nothing better than a bloody fight with other males and are brutally lustful and contemptuous in their attitude toward women.

The redness of Mars spoke to the ancient world of danger, fire, blood and anger. To the Babylonians it represented carnage, plague and disaster, but to the Romans it symbolized protection against pests, storms and droughts.

The balanced Martian can make a success as an athlete, though in those sports that need tenacity and strength rather than delicacy and skill. Careers such as those of soldier and policeman will attract him, and in humbler walks of life he may find his fulfillment as a barber, butcher, mechanic, smith or other worker in metal.

Physiologically Mars rules the adrenals – which rouse the body to take action, to fight or flee, and which stimulate self-defense and self-activity – the muscles, red blood corpuscles, sympathetic nervous system, sex glands and urogenital systems and, partly, the kidneys. It governs energy and fluids flowing out from their sources and strengthens the body's immune system, mustering its resistance against disease. Martian subjects are liable to hot, red ills, such as burns and scalds, fevers, inflammations, and wounds from blood-letting instruments.

The male biological symbol is used for Mars and is sometimes interpreted as a shield and spear, sometimes as initiative and objectivity (the arrow) springing from divine spirit (the circle). Mars rules in Aries and Scorpio, his houses are the first and eighth, his day is Tuesday and his hours are the third, tenth, seventeenth and twenty-fourth.

RIGHT Jupiter's chariot above the courtly activities of Church and State associated with the planet. The artist has mistakenly indicated on the front wheel that Pisces is one of Jupiter's "houses." They are in fact Cancer and, as indicated, Sagittarius.

JUPITER

Jupiter follows immediately upon Mars and is exemplified in the fifth of Shakespeare's seven ages of man.

> And then the justice,
> In fair round belly with good capon lin'd,
> With eyes severe and beard of formal cut,
> Full of wise saws and modern instances.

Shakespeare could scarcely have given a better picture of the Jupiter man, except possibly by writing "twinkling eyes" in the third line. For as Jupiter is the largest and, astrologically, the most beneficent planet, so his natives are mentally broad-minded, in the sense of ranging widely in thought and culture, and similarly physically large and benevolent toward their

as well as being expected to be by more mercurial characters. Since their ambitions are to move smoothly through life, in whatever professions they choose, towards their goals of achieving status through promotion duly earned by steady and consistent effort, to make money and to cut fine figures in the public regard, they like their times to be settled and free from threats of war or public disturbance.

Yet although they strive for every kind of material success and recognition, they are usually not materialistic. They try to recognize and eradicate the weaknesses in, and fully develop the capabilities of, their characters, and through their experience of living to attain spiritual maturity – for they are ambitious to understand the purpose of life and destiny Therefore they can be profound philosophers and theologians and, if they make the Church their vocation, become good fathers in God to their parishes as ordinary clergy and to their dioceses as bishops.

Nor are they selfish. They are humorous, in an affable rather than witty fashion (jovial is the adjective derived from

ABOVE A Roman bronze statuette (2nd to 4th centuries AD) of Zeus (Jupiter), holding a sceptre and thunderbolt.

fellows. Dignified to the point of being patriarchal even in early life (and thus apt to irritate their contemporaries with the middle-aged outlooks they adopt as early as their twenties – one cannot imagine them ever to have been young) they are natural leaders who expect to succeed and can be outstanding in any profession, earning high position and wealth, looking for respect and reverence as their due.

They are often good looking with an imposing, impressive manner, conventional in dress and behaviour, and fit thrones well whether in chairing the governing committees of clubs and societies or overseeing their peoples as emperors, kings and presidents.

They make good judges because they genuinely uphold what they consider best in the established order of laws, morals and religion.

Their innate conservatism may fail to move with the times, however, and they run the risk of actually being old-fashioned

BELOW A youthful, unbearded Jupiter with his "houses" of Pisces and Sagittarius, holding thunderbolts and a sceptre, presides over the activities of merchants.

ABOVE Here Jupiter accepts from Ganymede, the cup-bearer of the gods, a goblet of wine (to increase his joviality?). His chariot is drawn by peacocks, the birds associated with his queen, Juno.

Jove or Jupiter), and generous in appreciation of their friends and materially to causes they support. They have a marked social conscience, using their power to guard and protect the helpless and to console, encourage, preserve and heal those who need their assistance. As judges they would, wherever possible, temper the law with equity and mercy.

They are likely to inspire contempt and envy in those less able to cope with life for appearing too comfortable, prosperous and well fed, but they do not deserve this, for if good fortune is theirs, they have usually earned it, and if bad times come, they face them courageously. In desperate or hopeless conditions they display greater tenacity than average and retain optimism, even to the extent of being happy-go-lucky. Physically they are liable to stoutness, although they are usually healthy with it.

A negative Jupiter character is conceited, self-opinionated enough to consider that the world owes him a living, and prepared to act criminally to get what he thinks is due to him if the world happens not to agree with him. He will tend to exaggeration in speech, dress and demeanour, and become a larger-than-life, boastful, bombastic, extravagant braggadocio of a character.

The pituitary gland, which controls hormone production and performs a healing, harmonizing function in the body, is part of Jupiter's physical concern, as is the liver, which purifies the blood, and the body's fat with its protective and healing qualities. This last helps with the recovery of health after illness, but the stout man, although often a fine-looking and jolly fellow, may be predisposed to heart strain by carrying too much weight.

The symbol of Jupiter is sometimes said to represent his throne and is formed by a half-circle, representing mind and human spirit, rising above a cross (matter). It pictures spirit rising from and transcending worldliness and experience. Jupiter rules Sagittarius (positive and masculine) and Pisces (negative and feminine) and the ninth and twelfth houses. His day is Thursday and his best hours the fifth, twelfth and nineteenth.

SATURN

Saturn is the planet of the most negative aspects of the personality and is therefore considered malefic. If childhood and adolescence belong to Mercury, and mature middle age to Jupiter, Saturn's is the age of

the lean and slipper'd pantaloon,
With spectacles on nose and pouch on side:
His youthful hose, well sav'd, a world too wide
For his shrunk shank; and his big manly voice,
Turning again toward childish treble, pipes
And whistles in his sound.

BELOW The aged Saturn, bald, bent and carrying in his hand the scythe which is the emblem of death, "the Grim Reaper."

Saturnians, however, pass through all the ages of man just like the subjects of any other planet, and something of their qualities is necessary in every well-balanced human. They are cautious, controlled, patient, thrifty (with a risk of meanness), restrained, capable of hard work and great concentration, self-disciplined, mature and responsible. They are gifted with sobriety of both appetite and character (the "sober and godly matron" comes to mind as a description of the Saturnian lady) and pride themselves on their discretion, wisdom and resourcefulness. Their pessimistic nature leads them to expect the worst that fortune can bring, and they will insure against it by planning for every contingency.

In their personal relationships Saturnians strive to be fair, attributing to every man his due. But they often lose friends by their saturnine humour, which is often extremely intellectual but may be as biting as it is clever and cause offence by its satirical quality. In marriage the man will provide for his wife with scrupulous loyalty and concern, and the Saturnian woman will respond with an economic and conscientiously run household where everything will have a place and will be in that place.

The Saturnian has a wide choice of professions, provided that he can find departments in them where he can plan ahead and work routinely to a timetable at his own steady speed. He is liable to be a late developer and will therefore prefer a job into which he can fit at a humble level to begin with, and one which will give him time and opportunity to develop at his own pace. He wants steady advancement, no requirements that sudden decisions be made or inspiring leadership be provided by him, and a pension at the end. He needs time to bring his logic and clarity of thought to bear on concrete ideas and plans, which he prefers to abstract concepts. His gifts lie in sustaining monotonous, laborious work requiring patience, dedication and a sense of duty. He will do well in architecture and building, agriculture (he will enjoy its slow rhythms and the regularity of the cycle of seasons), the army (logistics and administration rather than leadership in the field), certain kinds of business, the public bureaucracy and politics, civil engineering, forestry, the Church and other contemplative occupations.

Rarely happy even at his best, the Saturnian character has it in him to make himself the most wretched of men. He feels external difficulties keenly, although he endures them patiently, but the internal problems are worse. His concern with self-discipline may make him introspective and aware of his faults. He often sees himself as unworthy and inadequate, a lonely failure, inhibited, limited and depressed. Such

ABOVE Here a less bleak and even grandfatherly Saturn presides over the autumnal activities associated with him. His chariot wheels bear the symbols of his "houses," Aquarius and Capricorn.

thoughts increase his natural dourness and melancholy and make him suspicious of his fellows. The negative aspects of the Saturnian's character may express themselves in malevolence and downright cruelty.

The influence in the horoscope of Saturn unrelieved by other planets is maleficent. It is the planet of ill-fortune, hardship, fear, sorrow, especially that of bereavement, and other loss, separation and suffering. It has to do with mental and physical limitation and confinement, including imprisonment, and the contraction of the quality of living by the hardening of arteries and other ills associated with old age.

The hard parts of the body – among others, bones and teeth – are ruled physiologically by Saturn. While imposing a necessary rigidity on the human frame, the skeleton and skull are emblems of death, which comes about by the Saturn-ian qualities of hardening and the gradual slowing down of the system which thus becomes increasingly bare, barren, dry and gaunt.

The symbol of Saturn, like that of death, may be regarded as a scythe or sickle, though he is sometimes portrayed as leaning on a crutch. Or, as has been seen in other planetary symbols, it is a cross (matter) over a half-circle (mind, human spirit), representing the limitation of the spiritual by the grossness of the physical, or the eventual and inevitable victory of death over every living physical organism. Saturn rules Capricorn and Aquarius and the tenth and eleventh houses. Its day is Saturday and its best hours the seventh, fourteenth and twenty-first.

URANUS

Uranus takes a long human lifetime of 84 years to complete one orbit round the sun and can therefore have little effect upon the individual. Some astrologers believe that the three planets discovered in the last two centuries had no influence at all on human life until they were discovered. But in spite of this belief, and the opinion that planets so distant and slow-moving must influence generations rather than single individuals, Uranus is believed to have some effect on those subjects in whose horoscopes it is prominent. They are said to be unconventional, possessing a strong drive to deviate from the normal, proud of their individuality, independence of mind and originality. Their impatience with old systems and accepted ideas, and their longing for freedom of expression and behaviour, often express themselves in rebelliousness against all authority and even in active revolution. In their personal lives they develop sexual and moral standards – or lack of them – irrespective of what Church, State and society might demand. They are versatile, inventive and strongly intuitive, with flashes of genius that suddenly produce in them insights of inspired creativeness which lead to advances in knowledge, especially scientific and technological. But they are not materialistic; there is something of the mystical in them, so that they are attracted to the occult and magical – it is not for nothing that astrologers sometimes describe themselves as "children of Uranus."

Their impatience with the caution of the Establishment and the lethargy of governments gives them a practical and strongly altruistic sense of brotherhood with the dispossessed and oppressed. In these days, when the troubles of the world – floods, famines, hurricanes, tornadoes, earthquakes, man-made disasters – are brought into their very homes, Uranians will be among the first to offer their services or dip into their pockets.

The negative qualities of the planet's subjects, besides those already mentioned, are once again their good ones in excess. It is easy for a frustrated reformer to cross the border into rebellion, or for one impatient with the *status quo* to demand that everything that appertains to it be disrupted and changed. The emphasis on freedom in their personal lives may lead to violent eccentricity, utter irresponsibility in family and social relationships, and perverted or depraved fanaticism.

Astrologers point out that since Uranus was discovered in 1781 the great rebellions and wars that have changed the world have taken place – the American War of Independence, the French and Russian revolutions, the liberation of the Spanish American states, the industrial, agricultural and

technological revolutions, the break-up of great empires into new and often powerful nation-states – and that the rapidity of change and development in the modern world has increased. These facts, they say, confirm the theory that Uranus influences movements rather than individuals.

The sympathetic nervous system has been assigned to Uranus physiologically and illnesses caused by its bad aspects resemble sudden revolutions – nervous breakdowns, cramps, hysteria, instability arising in adolescence or from the menopause, palpitations, paralysis, spasms and strokes. Homosexuality and sexual perversion are associated with it, but perhaps only because these subjects actively react against the conventional mores.

The planet was discovered by Herschel and first named after him, so its sign is his initial H surmounting the circle of divine spirit and completeness. Uranus is associated with Aquarius and the eleventh house but, like Neptune and Pluto and any other planet yet to be discovered, can have no day assigned to it.

NEPTUNE

BELOW Neptune, first discovered by Sir William Herschel (1738–1822), the Anglo-German astronomer, in 1781, photographed by the space probe Voyager.

Neptune takes nearly fifteen years to traverse a single sign of the zodiac and therefore affects individuals very little. Indeed, some authorities say that its influence becomes apparent only with death. Nevertheless, it is said to influence some uncommon characters and activities. Mesmerism, hypnotism, trances and mediumship come under its sway and, more ordinarily, a love of the sea which may lead to a risk of death by drowning. Musicians, artists and writers of certain types are among its subjects, as are idealistic humanists, mystics, sensitives and psychics. Its natives, with their subtle and other-worldly natures, susceptible to influences that do not touch more earthy individuals, seek to tap psychic or spiritual energies and power beyond the physical. Their natures expose them to many dangers. Their extreme sensitivity and physical and mental impressionability, besides making them impractical, vague and chaotic in their daily lives, render them inordinately vulnerable to suffering. The problems of other people and the horrors of the news to which we are all constantly exposed, and against which more ordinary people can mercifully steel themselves, drive the children of Neptune into the escapism of fantasy, daydreaming or the near madness of hallucination. In extreme cases they may try to shut out the abominations of life by taking refuge in drugs, alcohol and sedatives, or indulging their neuroses in sexual orgies and perversions, leading to the disintegration of their

LEFT A vigorous representation of Neptune. His chariot is drawn by fish-tailed white horses and he is smiled upon by Juno, accompanied by her peacock.

personalities and despair resulting in suicide. Their favourite weapons in destroying themselves are overdoses of their customary sedatives, or poison gas.

Astrologers point out that Neptune was discovered within a couple of years of the foundation of the modern spiritualist movement, usually dated from the manifestation of psychic phenomena at the home of the Fox family in Hydesville, New York, in 1848. The century and a half since then has seen the development of considerable interest in the scientific investigation of occult phenomena (the Society for Psychical Research was founded in 1882) and of major world spiritual movements. These include Pentecostalism, named as a third force in Christianity after Catholicism and Protestantism, the charismatic movement, and ecumenicalism – not only within Christianity in the World Council of Churches, but between the other great religions of the Earth.

Before the discovery of Neptune the government of the seas, and liquids generally, had been assigned to the Moon, but was then transferred to the new planet – mistakenly, it may be argued, since the influence of the Moon on the oceans is obvious. Physiologically Neptune rules the thalamus – that part of the brain which controls the aural and optic nerves – and the rhythms of growth, the spinal canal and some nervous and mental processes. Its negative effects include hysteria, insanity, mental and emotional disturbances, neuroses and obsessions, together with mysterious illnesses which in our present state of knowledge cannot be diagnosed. Neptune is characterized by a trident, represented by a half-circle (the human mind) transcending the cross of matter. Its zodiacal sign is Pisces and it is connected with the twelfth hour.

PLUTO

Pluto, in its orbital period of 248 years, moves far too slowly to relate to individual signs of the zodiac and needs to be seen in the context of the whole horoscope. Pluto was the god of death and the underworld and the planet named after him is that of death and destruction, representing the dark side of mankind. Astrologers claim that the almost exact coincidence of its discovery in 1930 with the rise of the Nazis (its influence is also powerful in Hitler's horoscope) was no accident. They also point out that the 1930s saw the climax of racketeering in the USA, a great period of lawlessness, and that international gangsterism in the shape of Hitler, Mussolini, Stalin and Hirohito, and many lesser luminaries of that ilk, flourished at the same time. The period was also that in which international enterprises began to come into prominence — worldwide business cartels, superpower politics, and cross-border movements and action groups like the Third International, fascist philosophy and the Mafia, all breaking out of their original national confines. The realization of their power by the masses, including the unions, mass demonstrations and sometimes mass hysteria, as at the Nuremberg Rallies, all make Pluto a planet potentially to be feared. Its influence continues today in various subcultures and the worldwide

ABOVE Lenin (1870–1924) and Stalin (1879–1953), architects of the Russian revolution that replaced the imperial rule of the Tsars with the Union of Soviet Socialist Republics.

BELOW Revolutionary movements throughout the world were marked by organized mass demonstrations such as those of the Nazi party at Nuremberg.

BELOW Benito Mussolini (1883–1945), founder of the Fascist movement in Italy.

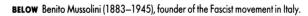

ABOVE Pluto, God of the Underworld, sits in majesty, accompanied by Cerberus, the three-headed guardian of the infernal regions.

Pluto represents the limits of the mind's consciousness, and is concerned with that underworld in the depths of our psyche which is involved with the occult in its literal sense of "hidden." It is the planet of the parapsychological, sometimes of neuroses caused by dissociation, or discordances creating rebellion against the wholeness of the character.

In mundane matters Pluto's subject is an individualist, interested primarily in success in attaining his objects. If he has a home and family he will be staunchly faithful to them, but mainly because he needs a firm base from which to launch his career, and will therefore need a partner who is ready to subserve him in this.

Pluto's physiological domain is in the renewing of cells to replace those in the body that die, the reproductive functions in their widest sense, and the creative and regenerative processes.

Its symbol, a capital P combined with a capital L, represents the initials of Percival Lowell, who calculated Pluto's position before it was actually observed. To those who prefer a more esoteric meaning it can also represent the circle of the human mind connected to the level of the subconscious, or of the forces below even that, the universal subconscious which Jung postulated as uniting humankind at the deepest level.

BELOW Pluto carrying off Persephone: a detail from the Red-Figure Volute Krater, ornate Apulian style, c380–370 BC, by the Iliupersis Painter.

organizations which supply them with drugs, international terrorism, large-scale demonstrations, and the waves of mindless violence which so affect modern societies. Other symptoms of Pluto's influence are said to be atomic power, with its threat of bringing death to all mankind; the menace of economic depression as advanced nations struggle with balance-of-payments deficits and the Third World is burdened with unpayable debts and seemingly willfully hit with every conceivable disaster; minorities terrorizing majorities and causing mayhem out of all proportion to their numbers in their attempts to achieve independence or their other aims through violence; and civil wars inspired by conflicting ideologies.

Pluto makes everything worse or, in its positive aspects, better than usual, and this is true of any striking personality in whose horoscope its influence is prominent. His power for good or evil can be immense. The eccentric orbit of the planet is symbolic of the depths or heights to which mankind is capable of sinking or soaring.

But even at its worst Pluto is not destructive of hope. It destroys in order to build afresh and eliminates to clear the ground for renewal. From Pluto's realm comes Proserpine, the goddess of spring, hope and new life. In the individual

CHARACTERISTICS OF THE HOUSES

FIRST HOUSE

This house concerns itself with the beginning and therefore the appearance of the subject as it strikes someone who meets him for the first time. It has to do with his childhood, the development of his personality, character and individuality, his general tendencies, those interests which concern him rather than others, and his tendencies to particular illnesses and his length of life.

Each house has a special relationship with a sign of the zodiac and one of the planets. The first house's sign is Aries and its planet Mars.

ABOVE The third house: communication and self-projection.

BELOW The first house: the first age of man, "the infant, mewling and puking in the nurse's arms."

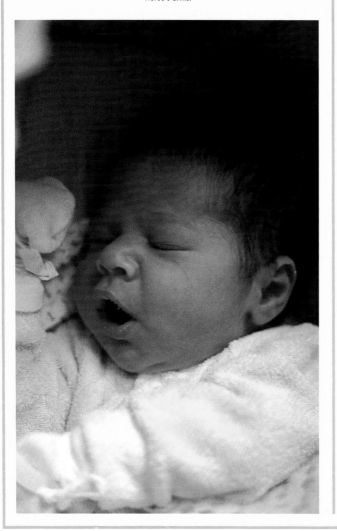

ABOVE The second house: possessions – how many people dream of having wealth enough to buy whatever they desire.

SECOND HOUSE

This is the domain of accumulated wealth (or lack of it), income, possessions, everything that makes the subject comfortable, contented and secure, and expenditure. This house has to do with the native's capabilities, resourcefulness and personal uniqueness. Its sign is Taurus and planet Venus.

THIRD HOUSE

The ability to communicate and make mental contact with others in conversation and in writing is dealt with here. Dependent on the quality of his capability to sell himself to others are an individual's relationships with his immediate environment, neighbours and relatives. Short journeys, such as the daily commuting to work which brings him into contact with others, are also the province of the third house, which has Gemini as its sign and Mercury as its planet.

LEFT The fourth house: affecting the actual dwelling places of the subject, and in a more abstract sense the bases from which he develops his life.

FOURTH HOUSE

This house is that of the home, both in the narrow sense of one's birthplace and dwelling places and also of one's native land. Real estate, buildings, property owned and rented, the physical bricks and mortar of the houses successively lived in by the native, the bases from which he develops his life, are included in this house's domain. It also has to do with the native's closing years in which he is preparing to depart. The sign is Cancer and the planet is the Moon.

FIFTH HOUSE

In the purview of this house are amusements, hobbies and pastimes, not only in the more trivial senses of entertainment, sport and pleasure, but recreation in the sense of practical and artistic creativity. It organizes the personal qualities and tastes of the subject into the image of himself he tries to project to others and governs his sex life, love affairs and children, both physical ones and the ideas which are his mind's children. Leo and the Sun are this house's sign and planet.

SIXTH HOUSE

Control of general health, physical conditions, the ability to work and all the factors that enable the native to fulfill his role in society and receive the service due to him from others are the subjects of this house. Its sign is Virgo, its planet Mercury.

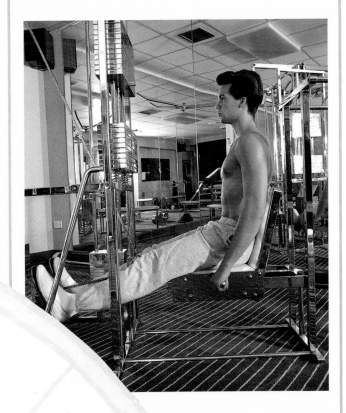

ABOVE The sixth house: physical well-being, fitness, in both senses, for life.

SEVENTH HOUSE

This has mainly to do with close relationships of the native's self with other people, particularly on the level of marriage; indications can be given here as to the type of spouse best suited to the subject's personality. Working relationships, business partnerships and also hostile confrontations in war or the law courts are governed by this house, whose sign is Libra and planet Mercury.

EIGHTH HOUSE

Here we find positive and negative influences. The former include help from others and the spiritual concerns of the subject. The latter cover loss and death and may suggest the manner of the native's own death. The death, however, may not be a physical demise but a radical transformation from former ways of thought to new ideas, or a complete change in profession and outlook. Matters to do with wills and legacies, resources shared with – or complete material dependence on – others, and self-sacrifice, come under the auspices of the house. Its sign is Scorpio, its planet Mars.

ABOVE. The eighth house: the cross, Christian symbol of death. In that tradition it also promises resurrection. Many astrologers believe in the post-mortem influence of the most distant planets.

NINTH HOUSE

The ninth house deals with travel – in both the physical sense of long journeys, and mental and spiritual voyaging into research, philosophy and religion. Higher education, the ferment and communication of ideas, the organizational side of the subject's Church or faith, are included, as are relationships with people not of the native's blood and with foreigners. The house's sign is Sagittarius, the planet Jupiter.

TENTH HOUSE

This is the domain of the native's occupations in life outside his home and immediate circle – the attainment or frustration in his career of ambition, fame or notoriety, and his public position, responsibilities and social status. Capricorn and Saturn are the sign and planet of the tenth house.

ABOVE. The seventh house: relationships of many kinds are the stuff of which life is made.. Children learn social living in the family and grow up to. establish associations outside it.

ELEVENTH HOUSE

Here are covered friends and group relationships and creative activities in societies, clubs and organizations of every kind. Ambitions for change and reform, sometimes unconventional, are also the province of the house, whose sign is Aquarius and planet either Saturn or Uranus.

TWELFTH HOUSE

This is the dwelling place of every kind of negative influence. All the obstacles in the way of fulfillment in life are here. Handicaps of ill-health or lack of personal attractiveness, barriers of class or education, any confinement such as imprisonment, hospitals, mental institutions, the monastic life, self-denying activities, withdrawal from reality into escapist fantasies, self-disintegration through drugs or drink, involvements that cut the individual off from normal life – such as membership of secret societies, terrorist groups or conspiracies – all these are the province of the twelfth house. Its sign is Pisces, its planet Jupiter or Neptune.

The first, fourth, seventh and tenth houses are known as "First" houses, the second, fifth, eighth and eleventh as "Succeedent" and the third, sixth, ninth and twelfth as "Cadent."

ABOVE The tenth house: personal ambition. The politician in full voice.

BOTTOM LEFT The ninth house: public figures engaged in public prayer – the organizational side of their faith.

BELOW The twelfth house: disintegration and exclusion.

CHAPTER FOUR

INTERPRETATION

Having mastered the vocabulary, grammar and symbolism of astrology, the interpreter of a horoscope has then to adopt a system whereby he omits no important feature of the chart. There are many astrological "cookbooks" which summarize the characteristics of a subject with, for example, the sun in Pisces, the moon in Aquarius and Jupiter in the fifth house, and a good deal of help and general guidance can be obtained from these but the really capable astrologer is the one who develops that insight which will enable him to understand intuitively and instinctively every chart he draws. The process is similar to the comprehension of any art. A musician learns theory and composition as well as the practical technique of playing his chosen instrument; a writer grasps vocabulary and grammar and develops style; a painter masters composition, perspective, design and skill in using his media. Most of them can become adequate in their chosen art by practice, application and perseverance. A very few with genius will become literary giants or great masters.

There are many methods of interpretation and every individual must develop his own. The following technique is merely a guide. Whatever method the student evolves, he must make sure that he has included every item needed for a complete reading. The interpreter should not be surprised to discern many apparent contradictions and inconsistencies. He is allegedly studying the character of a human who is born, as we all are, with a mass of potentialities of which circumstances will allow only a few to be fully developed, appetites which social pressures will control, and desires

ABOVE *An Astrologer* by Cornelius Bega (1631–1664). Pictures such as this built up the occult mystique of astrology.

Saturne	Jupiter	Mars	Sol	Venus	Mercure	Luna
Saturday	Thursday	Tuesday	Sunday	Friday	Wenfday	Wunday

ABOVE The days of the weeks shown in the order of the supposed (Aristotelian) distances of the planets from the earth: Saturn furthest, "Luna" nearest.

which will often pull the subject in different directions as he moves through life.

Having noted the various elements in the character, the interpreter's second step is to work out their comparative strengths. The subject may then learn to integrate his personality by nurturing his positive qualities and disciplining, even eradicating, his weaknesses and interior incompatibilities.

The third step is to write a complete interpretation including all the information gleaned from the many elements present in the chart. It should be emphasized once again that an astrologer is not a prophet. His business is not to tell fortunes or foretell the future. In interpreting the trends of the subject's future he is not unlike a weather forecaster who can approximately tall from the behaviour of the atmosphere that the conditions will be fine or stormy in a given area.

The following method is one among many. The student may list:

1. General features from (a) the lunar modes; (b) the characteristics, positive and negative, of the planets (Neptune, Uranus and Pluto may be excluded), the ascendant and the MC from the signs in which they are placed; (c) the triplicities (sometimes called trigons); (d) the quadruplicities; (e) main aspect patterns.

2. The ascendant sign.

3. The ascendant ruler in its sign and house.

4. The Sun in its sign and house. (If Leo is in the ascendant this will be the same as **3**.).

5. The Moon in its sign and house. (If Cancer is in the ascendant this will be the same as **3**.).

6. Angular planets, ie those within an 8° orb of conjunction with the ascendant, MC, descendant and IC.

7. The individual planets.

8. The aspects – of planets to each other and to the ascendant and MC.

Following these steps in our specimen horoscope, we have:

1. (a) The lunar nodes are in the eleventh and fifth houses.

(b) Four of the planets are in positive signs, three are in negative. The ascendant is in a positive sign, the MC in a negative.

(c) Two planets are in fire signs, one in earth, two in air and two in water.

(d) Of the quadruplicities, three planets occupy cardinal signs, one a fixed and three a mutable (common) sign.

(e) Aspect patterns. The Sun, Mercury and Uranus are all in conjunction, as are Venus and Pluto; Jupiter and Neptune are in opposition, and both form T-squares with the Sun and Mercury; Mars is square to Saturn and Jupiter square to Uranus; The Moon is in trine with Neptune: the strongest patterns. Moderate are the sextile aspects of the Moon with

Jupiter and Pluto, and weak are the semi-square aspect of the Sun and Mars, the semi-sextiles of Mercury and Pluto and of Venus with Saturn, and the sesquiquadrate of Jupiter and Pluto. Relationships of the planets with the ascendant and the MC include four oppositions, one sextile, two squares, one conjunction and one trine and one semi-sextile.

2. The ascendant sign is Aries.

3. The ascendant ruler is Mars, which is in Gemini and the third house.

4. The Sun is in Cancer and the third house.

5. The Moon is in Gemini and the second house.

6. The angular planets are Jupiter in Aries and the twelfth house; Neptune in Libra and the seventh house; the Sun and Uranus in Cancer and the third house; and Mercury, also in Cancer but the fourth house.

7. Already noted are Mars (**3.** above), the Sun (**4.**), the Moon, Jupiter, Neptune, Uranus and Mercury. There remain Venus, Saturn and Pluto. Venus and Pluto are both in Leo in the fifth house, Saturn is in Virgo in the sixth house.

8. The aspect patterns have been listed under **1.** (*e*.)

Following is one general interpretation of the Harrow woman's data (see page 26). Other students would find different emphases and even different fundamental meanings and readers may like to make their own analyses. A much more detailed reading could be given – but print is not elastic.

ANALYSIS

1. (*a*) The north node of the moon in the eleventh house indicates some unexpected and unearned advantage from acquaintances and, possibly, from the native's creative activities, or some change of occupation or direction in later life.

The south node in the fifth house could indicate frustration in the subject's creative ambitions. Since speculation is one concern of this house, there is a warning that the subject should be careful in such matters as investment.

(*b*) The Moon, Venus, Mars and Jupiter are in positive signs; the Sun, Mercury and Saturn in negative. This pattern indicates a character who uses her instincts and intuitions rather than her intellect and reason in responding to the challenges of life. She has a loving and expansive nature, an optimistic view of existence, powerful emotions and no lack of assertiveness. On the negative side there is a danger of tactlessness, possible intolerance and distrust of the self under an appearance of confidence.

(c) The equal distribution of signs represents a well-balanced character: enough "earth" to keep her feet on the ground and sufficient of the others for an equal development of emotions, mental activity, intuition and energy.

(d) Again there is a balance: qualities of leadership, steadiness and assertiveness are modified by some self-doubt and inclination to change direction in life. The subject has enough common sense to be careful about such changes and not to allow fantasies or discontents to sweep her into them.

(e) The interpretation of the aspects is given below.

2. The interpreter should read afresh the traits attributed to any sign and planet in Chapters Two and Three as he works, and allow his mind to develop a "feel" for the strands that are making up the composition of the character he is studying. The ascendant sign, being Aries, *by itself* suggests impulsiveness, enthusiasm and aggressiveness as dominant factors in this subject's character.

3. The ascendant ruler in sign and house is Mars in Gemini and the third house, which may be summarized as dealing with intelligence, communications and near relations. The force of Mars and the restlessness of Gemini can result in impatience and intolerance in the subject's mind, finding expression in a brusqueness of speech that may offend and can cause disruption in family life.

BELOW A diagram showing the effects of the signs of the zodiac on the human body. From Athanasius Kircher's *Ars Magna Lucis et Umbrae*, Amsterdam, 1671.

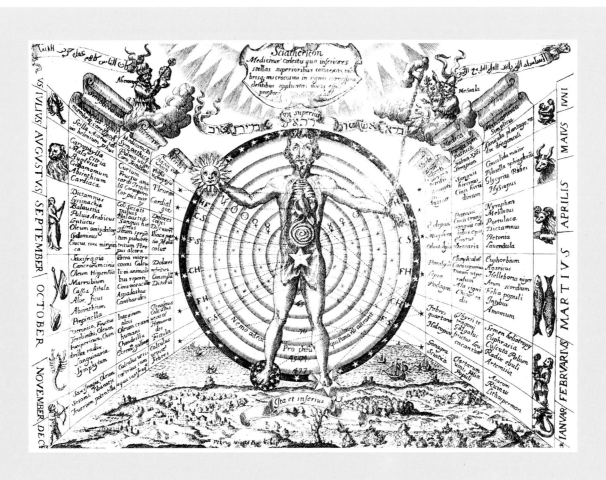

4. The Sun in Cancer betokens a good memory, sharp ear and a talent for mimicry. These talents, combined with features of the third house, which include communication with others, could mean a career on the stage, in public speaking or in writing. The subject may well have an ability to write the kind of vivid correspondence to her relations and close friends that they keep for their sheer interest.

5. The Moon in Gemini shows itself in nervousness and restlessness which may result in talkativeness, either because the subject is full of opinions which she has to express or because she is concerned with helping to mend unhappy relationships of people within her circle. The second house concerns wealth, possessions and finance and the subject should probably be careful not to talk or give her confidence carelessly to possibly corrupt financial advisers.

6. Planets that are angular, ie within an orb of 8° of the ascendant, MC, descendant and IC, have a stronger influence on the horoscope than some others, and particular notice should therefore be taken of them.

Here Jupiter is in Aries and the twelfth house, Jupiter, the planet of optimism and expansiveness, tempers the energy and aggressiveness of Aries and makes for a character that can lead with wisdom and a balanced judgment. The leadership may be of an inspiring kind in social, educational or religious movements. The negative side of the Jupiter–Aries combination is a temptation to be concerned with self, to be over-confident on one's vision of truth and to boost it intolerantly and impatiently against the insight of others. Jupiter is one of the planets that rules the twelfth house, the most negative of all the houses, and his "angular" strength could heighten the difficulties the native may experience in expressing and fulfilling her ideals. She may find herself confined by the dead weight of the Establishment and there is again the possibility of misfortune in the careless spending of money or the waste of personality in the struggle to achieve satisfaction.

The seventh house is that of close relationships, especially marriage, and Neptune in Libra indicates a change in direction in the subject's attitude to what is important in life, and a

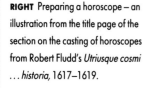

RIGHT Preparing a horoscope – an illustration from the title page of the section on the casting of horoscopes from Robert Fludd's *Utriusque cosmi ... historia*, 1617–1619.

development of the sense of social responsibility. Libra is the ruler of the seventh house and strengthens this tendency. The sign is one of maturity and indicates that the change happens in the prime of life.

The influence of the Sun in Cancer (see **4.** above) is strengthened by its angular position.

Uranus in Cancer symbolizes the break with home and also the tendency of the subject for individual and original planning of her own home. Uranus deals with the occult and the spiritual and the third house with the ability to communicate with others, so the home might well contain a room set aside for a ministry of healing of body or spirit, or as a chapel or meditation room.

Mercury in Cancer strengthens the development of the retentive memory mentioned above, but also the tendency of the subject to be swayed by her emotions. This in turn could reinforce the disposition to subjectivity in judgment and prejudice in opinions which has already been mentioned. Cancer is the sign of the fourth house and its presence here shows the native's strong affection for her home, both as the family abode and as the material house.

7. Venus in Leo in the fifth house emphasizes the strong social sense of the subject. She loves entertaining. The combination of planet, sign and house here indicates an ardent and faithful lover and a loving mother of her children, but with a bent towards possessiveness and jealousy. Pluto is so far distant and slow moving that its influence on individual characters and lives is unobservable.

8. The individual aspects

(1) ⊙☌☿ (good influence – benasp). This combination is one of power, vitality and liveliness of intellect.

(2) ⊙♇♀ (bad influence – malasp). An aspect of minor significance, implying some emotional weakness that may result in certain unsatisfactory personal relationships.

(3) ⊙□♃ and ⊙□♆ (malasp). The T-squares of these three planets reinforce the danger of intolerance which appears in other parts of this horoscope. This is a characteristic due not so much to confidence in the rightness of the subject's opinions as to frustration and her vulnerability to the sufferings of the world. If her own life were to be unhappy, she could become morbidly sensitive to these miseries and furiously impatient with the failure of other people's efforts to solve the problems of mankind. Even with a secure background the intolerance arising out of her very idealism will never be far from the surface.

(4) ⊙ ♅ (benasp). The markedly positive qualities of

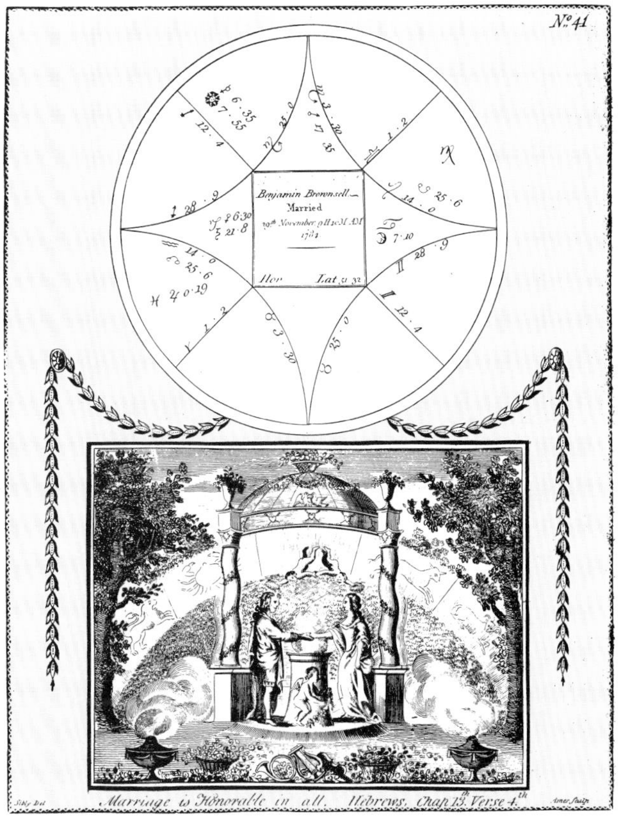

ABOVE Chart of a marriage in 1732 of an old, rich bridegroom to a young, poor bride, which E Sibley, an astrologer, phrophesied would fail. The bride left after one night.

the Sun are guided into unconventional paths by the influence of Uranus. Impatience with the status quo, though balanced by other elements in the chart, will always be present under the surface and the subject will take pride in thinking for herself.

(5) ⊙ MC (malasp). As the MC symbolically stands for the summit or climax of the individual life and the powerful Sun is in opposition, this relationship suggests considerable struggles for the subject and possibly personal failure in the attainment of her aims.

(6) ☽*♃ (benasp). The subject's affection for her family, cultivation of the spiritual side of her nature, disciplining of the faults of which she is conscious and attempts to attain spiritual maturity will go far to meet the weaknesses and handicaps of other aspects. The storms in her life can be met by a cultivation of "that peace which the world cannot give."

(7) ☽△♆ (benasp). This relationship reveals a mystical, intuitive streak in the character which is a good counterpoise to its outward vivacity, assertiveness and authority.

(8) ☽*♇ (benasp). The subject has the capacity to respond to conditions, to eliminate errors and to accept transformation. This means that she can discipline herself (not necessarily that she will!) against the impatience and intolerance which are part of her very idealism. It is likely that her instincts will guide her subconscious to know when she is at fault – it is the conscious facing up to shortcomings that may prove difficult.

(9) ☽* Ascendant (benasp). Early ideals will mature as life passes and not disappear. Cultivating and being faithful to them will help to lighten the darkness if the difficulties threatened by (3) and (5) above materialize.

(10) ☽⊼ (benasp). This is a reinforcement of (9). Even when things are at their darkest there will be some joys to compensate.

(11) ☿□♃ and ☿□♆ (malasp). This is another pattern of T-squares and represents a gloomy side of the character which could surface if the subject's life were submitted to extreme tension. The strength and idealism of the intellect could give way to superficiality, extravagance of behaviour and opinion, or the finding of refuge in fantasy. Again there is a risk of despair caused by over-sensitivity to the sufferings of the world.

(12) ☿ ♂ ♅ (benasp). There is here a lively originality of thought, spiritual rather than intellectual.

(13) ☿ ⊻ ♇ (benasp). This is a slight confirmation of (8) where the instinct guides the subject in the direction of transformation and regeneration.

(14) ☿□ ascendant (malasp). There is an indication here of a parting of the ways, in that the beginning of life pointed in one direction whereas the subject developed along another, harder path.

(15) ☿□ MC (malasp). Once again there is a suggestion of struggle in that the subject's habits of thought will in some way conflict with the fulfillment of her aims.

(16) ♀ ⊻ ♄ (benasp). There is a tendency here to treat personal relationships cautiously – once bitten, twice shy? – but it is not strong.

(17) ♀ ♂ ♇ (benasp). Here the love and joy that are the properties of Venus are tinged with the elimination and transformation that are Pluto's domain. The subject has, through not always happy experience, learned to love truly.

(18) ♂□♄ (malasp). The assertiveness of Mars combines badly with Saturn's limitations to produce unhappy situations for the subject. This relationship could indicate a development in her of ideas which are unacceptable in the milieu in which she works, and which are suppressed or opposed by its more orthodox members.

(19) ♃□♅ (malasp). Another square! The optimism and expansiveness that are Jupiter's can be neutralized, once again by opposition aroused by the unconventional nature of the subject's thought.

(20) ♃♂♆ (malasp). Here Jupiter's "joviality" is once more countered, this time by the overwhelming sense of the world's miseries that Neptune can inspire in those who are over-sensitive to them.

(21) ♃⊡♇ (malasp). There is here a very slight influence of a consciousness of mortality that destroys joy, a sense of the pathos that underlies all life, perhaps doubt and self-distrust which the subject fights and mostly suppresses in herself.

(22) ♃ ♂ ascendant (benasp). The subject's natural disposition from the beginning of her life was optimistic and happy.

(23) ♃□ MC (malasp). Again there comes the element of frustration in the attainment of aims and fulfillment of ideals.

(24) ♅♂MC (malasp). The unconventional streak in the subject again frustrates her.

(25) ♆♂ ascendant (malasp). Neptune, which in this horoscope has several times exposed the subject's sensitive nature to an overwhelming sense of the world's unhappiness, here directly conflicts with the strong influence of Jupiter's optimism at the beginning of her life. She has the weapon of innate happiness to fight the awareness of miseries about which she can do very little. Consequently she can steel herself against them without being overwhelmed by guilt. But depression may sometimes need to be fought hard.

(26) ♇△ ascendant (benasp). Positive Pluto makes everything better. Here the planet of the end of things meets the subject's beginning. This suggests that at the end of her life, in spite of the struggles and frustrations, she will feel that having remained loyal to the truth as she sees it, she will have conquered – even if apparently frustrated in her aims.

Of the 28 aspects listed above (two each under 3 and 11) 14 include Uranus, Neptune and Pluto. In many personal horoscopes the interpreter would omit these references.

SUMMARY

We have here a well-balanced personality, innately happy and secure, with qualities of leadership that could inspire those who follow her. She is a good communicator in speech and writing. She possesses a lively, independent intellect, blessed with a good memory. This can develop strong, unconventional opinions which the subject will seek to propagate

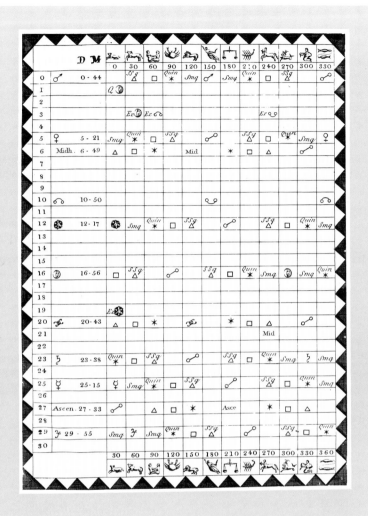

Table of aspects at the nativity of George Witchell, astronomer, born 21 March, 1728, from E Sibley's *Illustration of the Celestial Art of Astrology*, 1817.

energetically and which are likely to arouse opposition. Her case will not be helped by her impatience with what she might interpret as the lack of vision and imagination of her opponents and she risks being driven into tactlessness and intolerance in her presentation of what she is confident is right. She may be involved in considerable struggle and may well be frustrated in her ultimate aims. She must be careful to cultivate open-mindedness so as to appreciate the sincerity of those who oppose her, and not to react so strongly to criticism that she becomes entrenched in prejudice.

Another danger would appear to be financial. There is no hint of materialism in her chart and as one who has little interest in money she must avoid the danger of trusting inefficient or dishonest financial advisers. She needs to employ completely trustworthy counsellors in this field and avoid

speculation herself. Her emotions are powerful and her relationships on the whole happy, especially those within her close family. She is a homemaker, with a tendency to possessiveness – she may find it hard to let her children go when they reach an age at which they begin to think and plan for themselves. In wider circles she is sociable and enjoys communicating formally and informally.

There is considerable sensitivity to the sufferings of the world and a sense of guilt that she is secure and happy. Such sensitivity could make her extremely vulnerable if the circumstances of her own life should become unhappy.

Her mystical, intuitive streak which can express itself in religious activity or in mysteries more arcane. She is likely to feel, at the end of her life, whatever her successes or failures, that she has been true to herself and her ideals.

CHAPTER FIVE

A BRIEF HISTORY OF ASTROLOGY

ABOVE An imaginary view of Babylon where, together with Sumer, the foundations of astrology were laid.

Astrology began over 5,000 and possibly as much as 7,000 years ago, the first exact science to be studied by mankind. It was, to begin with, a royal and national science. In Ur of the Chaldees, a city of Sumer, that part of Mesopotamia immediately north of the Persian Gulf where astrology was probably born, it was confined to divining the omens for king and nation only. North of Sumer was Babylonia and in those two countries were laid the foundations of the study from which the modern systems have descended.

The fixed constellations seemed unchanging, but in the clear atmosphere of Mesopotamia, where observation was assisted by wide expanses of flat landscape, the movement of those heavenly bodies which seemed to traverse regular paths

ABOVE On this cylinder seal of the Scribe Adda, *c*2400–2200 BC is pictured, among other deities, the Sun-God, Shamash (on the right).

LEFT A Chinese zodiacal vase of the 5th to 6th centuries AD decorated with the images of 12 animals representing the months of the year.

ABOVE A Babylonian boundary stone, c1120 BC, recording a gift of land, bears the symbols of gods invoked to protect the deed.

in the skies was noticed, and the planets we call Mercury, Venus, Mars, Jupiter and Saturn were known to the Sumerians, the Babylonians and their successors. The belt of the zodiac in which the paths of the planets mainly lay (though they occasionally wandered outside it, when they were thought to be resting in their "houses") may have been known for millenia, though most modern scholarship ascribes its recognition to Greek science of the sixth and fifth centuries BC. The Sumerians identified Venus with Innin or Inanna, the Lady of Heaven, and the Babylonians regarded her as Ishtar, goddess of war and carnage in her appearance as the Morning Star, but of love, procreation, fertility, gentleness and luxury when she shone as the Evening Star. She was the daughter of Sîn, the Moon god, and sister of Utu or Shamash, deity of the Sun. Nergal, god of war and destruction, and ruler of the underworld, was appropriately the red planet, Mars; Mercury was Babylonian Nabu; Jupiter was Marduk and Saturn Ninib.

Reports of earthly phenomena apparently resulting from the movements of heaven's gods, though most of them were on the level of meteorological forecasts, were recorded in writings known as the Enuma Anu Enlil tablets, dating from the beginning of the fourth millenium BC Records of predictions followed, first of events such as wars and floods, later birth horoscopes of individual kings, some of which still exist on cuneiform tablets.

Eastwards, Mesopotamian astrology penetrated to India around the sixth century BC and to China and Indo–China soon after (though there may have been some earlier influence).

Westwards it travelled to Egypt and Greece. Primitive peoples in western Europe, independently of Sumer and Babylon, had learned as early as 2000 BC to mark the solstices and other astronomical events by systems of megaliths. In Mexico, from about 300 AD, the Mayas developed an even more accurate knowledge of astronomy than the Babylonians, evolving a calendar of 365 days and a zodiac of thirteen signs. The Aztecs produced a somewhat cruder system.

LEFT A Mayan manuscript from Mexico. In the clear atmosphere of their location, the Mayas developed a sophisticated astronomical system.

THE IMPORTANT EARLY TEXTS

The Greeks identified the planets with deities very similar in character to those of the Babylonians. Ishtar, the Morning and Evening Star, became Aphrodite, in Roman culture Venus. Nabu turned into Greek Hermes, Roman Mercury, messenger of the gods. Through the conquests of Alexander the Great (356–323 BC) Greek ideas spread throughout the ancient world, but the Greeks themselves were exposed to foreign influence. In 280 BC Bedosus, a Chaldean priest, brought astrology to Greece.

Egypt, however, had developed her own astronomy long before. From possibly 2000 BC she had developed a calendar which the Greeks later made their own. The Persians introduced astrology to Egypt in the sixth century BC, with the result that the Egyptians evolved a form of astral religion which eventually influenced both Greece and Rome. Thirty-six stars named decans were selected, rising at ten-day intervals, each governed by a spirit. The ten-day periods evolved into ten-degree subdivisions of the twelve 30° zodiacal signs. In about 150 BC a treatise by a fictitious priest, Petosiris, and king, Nechepso, ascribed each day of the week to a planet.

CLAUDIUS PTOLEMY, GEOGRAPHER, ASTRONOMER AND ASTROLOGER

ABOVE Ptolemy (Claudius Ptolemaeus), 2nd century AD, astronomer, geographer and mathematician, established the theory accepted until the 15th century that the earth was the centre of the universe.

RIGHT A scribe presenting a copy of the *Tetrabiblos,* by Ptolemy, to King Henry VI. Ptolemy's theory of the motion of the celestial spheres has had a profound and permanent effect upon astrology.

At Alexandria the Greek astronomer Ptolemy composed the Almagest or Tetrabiblos ("Four Books"), the first extant definitive astrological treatises. In them he taught that the world is surrounded by the "Ambient," power derived from aetherial nature. Forces from the heavenly bodies transmitted through this medium affect procreation, fertility, processes of growth and the forms of developing creatures. Calculations of the future positions of the stars and planets were accordingly believed to make predictions possible, enabling the knowledgeable physician to cure illnesses. Ptolemy classified stars into "benefics" and "malefics," producing good and evil according to their positions and relationships with others, and listed the characteristics of the zodiacal signs and the houses. After applying his theory to nations and cities, he extended it to individuals. Through him the Greeks brought astrology into the province of the common man.

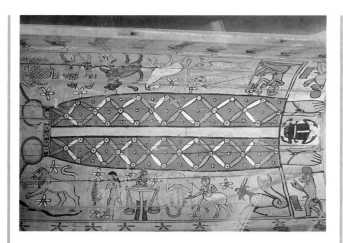

The interior of an Egyptian coffin, 2nd century AD, showing the goddess Nut and the signs of the zodiac.

Even more important was the collection of texts made between 50 BC and 150 AD, attributed to Hermes, the Greek Mercury and Egyptian Thoth. That ordinary though well-to-do men were concerned with astrology is shown by the fact that horoscopes were sometimes inscribed on tombs.

The Chinese were probably the first people to develop astronomy apart from astrology, which they used to forecast events. They divided the sky into five "palaces," a central region round the pole and four equatorial divisions corresponding to the four seasons. Twelve signs – Tiger, Hare, Dragon, Serpent, Horse, Sheep, Monkey, Hen, Dog, Pig, Rat and Ox – alternatively possessing the quality of positive *Yang* (masculinity, light and motion) and negative *Yin* (femininity, darkness and repose), were based on divisions of the equator (not of the sky, as with the zodiac).

The complicated and apparently scientific system that was to be the ancestor of European astrology was meanwhile being developed by the Greeks from their own genius combined with Babylonian and Egyptian elements. Philosophy, medicine and religion all supported it. The Stoic doctrine of universal "sympathy" between the microcosm (man) and the macrocosm (the universe) – expressed in the dictum used later when Stoicism no longer existed, "as above, so below" – and astrology seemed made for each other. Mithraism, so great a rival of Christianity that a toss of the historical coin might have made it, rather than Christianity, the religion of Europe, initiated its worshippers – who in their rites wore masks representing the animals of the zodiac – into successive mysteries representing the soul's journey through the seven planetary realms. Gnosticism in its many forms and some of

the mystery religions were based on very similar concepts. Melothesis, the "science" that teaches that the stars and zodiac dominate parts of the body, became part of standard medical practice.

In Rome the official augurs opposed astrology when it arrived there during the second century BC, but the populace welcomed "Chaldeans" who told their fortunes by the stars. The Roman emperors disliked astrology, regarding it as a possible weapon to be used by would-be usurpers of their thrones. It found a supporter in the person of the Neoplatonist philosopher Plotinus, who settled in Rome in 241 AD.

A 17th-century Chinese painting of a group studying the yin-yang symbol.

In spite of a number of references in the Old Testament to astrology, Judaism had little time for it even though it recorded the fact that "the stars in their courses fought against" Sisera. According to Christianity, Judaism's largest and most successful heresy, the coming of Christ broke the control of the planets over human fate. One Christian view was that the star of Bethlehem changed the old order; another that it was the constellation of Cassiopeia, which produced an unusually bright star every 300 years and was known to the ancients as

ABOVE The birth of Jesus announced to the shepherds by a host of angels and the Star of Bethlehem. Astrology is of course immediately relevant to the Christian dilemma concerning predestination and free will.

"The Woman with Child." Furthermore, Cassiopeia was the presiding constellation of Syria/Palestine, and it was natural for the Magi – who were astrologers, not kings – to follow the sign that proclaimed to them that a woman of Palestine had brought forth a royal son.

KARMA

In India the Hindu Vedas, sacred scriptures written before 1000 BC, allegedly by the seven Rishis or Shining ones, the stars of the Great Bear, were influenced by Babylonian astrology. Individual horoscopes came into fashion following Greek influence after the conquests of Alexander the Great. India nevertheless developed her own system, expanding the lunar mansions – the *Nakshatras* – more fully than any other country. Hinduism added to astrology the idea of Karma (the results that a man's actions bring upon himself during the whole of his existence) and reincarnation. The stars could reveal the effects of every deed of past incarnations and the present life, together with future actions of this life and existences yet to come, and indicate the stage in his spiritual development attained by an individual.

India takes astrology seriously today. Only about a dozen learned astronomer astrologers are allowed the prestigious title of Jyotisha Pandit. They publish an annual almanac called *Panchaga*. The police use astrologers in their work, and auspicious days are chosen for important enterprises – the erection of private houses or public buildings, the days on which medical operations should be performed, a child should be conceived or a householder move house. Indian astrologers are said to have predicted the outbreaks of both World Wars and the downfall of Hitler.

Early Christianity was sometimes tolerant of, sometimes hostile to, astrology. *The Clementine Recognitions* (second century) stated that God created the celestial bodies to be an indication of things past, present and future and that Abraham had recognized the creator from the stars. Hostile Christian writers, including Augustine, attacked astrology with a double-edged sword of an argument – it was either erroneous or, if right, owed its accuracy to the devil.

The Jewish *Sepher Yetsirah* (Book of Creation, written *c*.500 AD), one of the classics of the Jewish mystical system known as the *Kabbalah*, and the *Zohar* (Book of Splendor) both affected European thought and both revealed faith in celestial influence.

Astrology all but disappeared in Europe during the Dark Ages but was kept alive by the Mohammedans. In the eighth century the Caliph Al Mansur founded a school of astrology in Baghdad with the practical aims of catching thieves, recovering lost possessions and determining the best time to start enterprises. When learning revived in the eleventh and twelfth centuries Christendom accepted Arabian astrological treatises because of their Aristotelian flavour. Aquinas (*c*. 1126–1274)

ABOVE Paracelsus (Theophrastus Bombastus von Hohenheim) (c1490–1541), physician and alchemist, believed that, since mankind is penetrated by the astral spirit, doctors must understand and use astronomy.

gave the definitive Christian compromise with astrology and made it acceptable. Since the stars influence human appetites, which few men can resist, their forecasts are mostly correct; but those morally strong enough to resist can negate their predictions.

Astrology/astronomy (for the two did not really part company until the seventeenth century), reached its zenith during the Renaissance, when the New Learning (of which much was old rediscovered) permeated to the masses. Famous scholars wrote astrological treatises, of whom the most eminent was the Swiss Paracelsus (1492–1541) who believed that man's inner nature corresponded to the universe. He could, however, resist the influence of stars and planets.

Some popes (for example Julius II, Leo X and Paul III) and potentates favoured astrologers. Catherine de Medici patronized the famous Nostradamus (1503–1566), and Elizabeth I of England Dr John Dee (1527–1608).

BELOW Nostradamus predicting the fate of French kings to Catherine de Medici by means of a magic mirror.

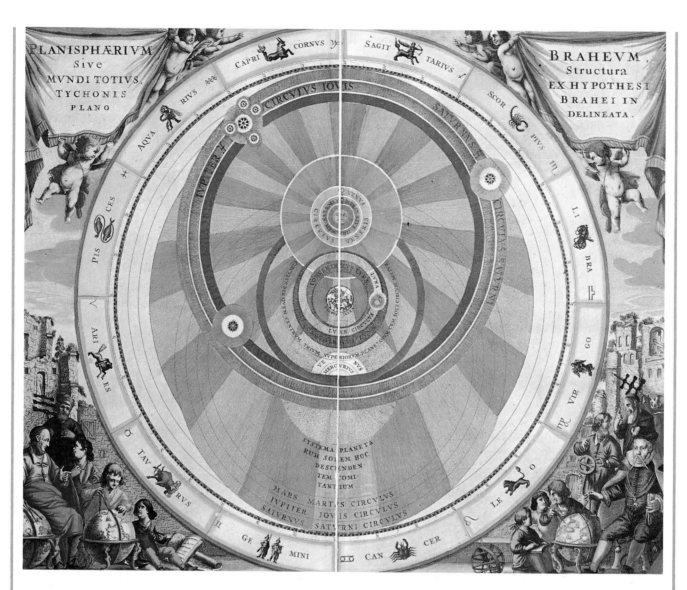

ABOVE An illustration of the geo-heliocentric universe of Tycho Brahe (1546–1601), b December 14 (Capricorn), Danish astronomer and cataloger of the stars.

SCIENTIFIC CHALLENGES

The discovery by Copernicus (1473–1543) that the earth was not the center of the universe but traveled round the Sun, and the development of the beginnings of modern astronomy by Tycho Brahe (1546–1601), Kepler (1571–1630) and Galileo (1564–1642), inventor of the telescope, did not destroy astrology, though it was undermined. In spite of strong condemnation by Pope Urban VIII in 1631, a priest, Placidus de Titis, was the most famous astrologer of the seventeenth century and by the publication of *Physiomathematica sive Coelestis Philosophia* became the father of modern astrology.

The science was kept alive in England by men of considerable intellectual repute, such as William Lilly (1602–1681) who in 1648 so successfully prophesied the Great Fire of London in 1666 that a Parliamentary committee investigated him to see if he had started the blaze. Popular interest in astrology was maintained by the publication of annual astrological almanacs but the intellectual climate of the Age of Enlightenment rejected astrology as a superstition, and Sir William Herschel's discovery of Uranus in 1781 almost dealt the science a death blow by destroying the planets' mystical number, seven, arguing that all calculations on the basis of the hitherto known planets were worthless.

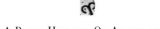

However, Ebenezer Sibley published his *Science of Astrology* in 1790, reissued in 1812 and 1828, and an astro-medical text book *The Key to Physick and the Occult Science*. Enlightenment also produced a reaction of faith which expressed itself in religious movements such as the Methodist revival, and in occultism. James Wilson's *A Complete Dictionary of Astrology* appeared in 1819. Robert Cross–Smith (1795–1832) in 1827 launched *The Prophetic Messenger* under the name of Raphael, still published as *Raphael's Almanac, Prophetic Messenger and Weather Guide*. The 1824 Vagrancy Act in England actually made fortune-telling by the stars a punishable offence.

ABOVE The Trial of Galileo at Rome, 1633, instigated by Pope Urban VIII. His "crime" was the discovery that the earth was not the center of the universe. Galileo was forced publicly to deny the truth.

ABOVE The Great Fire of London (1666), so successfully forecast by the astrologer William Lilly that he was suspected of starting the blaze.

ASTROLOGY IN THE 20TH CENTURY

Intense interest in spiritualism, psychical research and charismatic esoteric forms of religion was current in the second part of the nineteenth century, probably as a reaction against the growing scientific materialism. Madame Blavatsky's foundation of the Theosophical Society in 1875, appealing to intellectuals, revived interest in astrology among other beliefs. Annie Besant, Blavatsky's successor, ardently believed in it and the Theosophical Society Astrological Lodge, founded in 1920, issues a quarterly, *Astrology*, and gives courses and awards diplomas. Foulsham's *Old Moore's Almanac*, with a continuous existence under different names since the eighteenth century, and sold between the two World Wars for a penny, was widely circulated. At the other extreme the scholarly Faculty of Astrological Studies, founded in 1948, runs training courses and awards certificates, diplomas, scholarships and medals to serious students of astrology.

In France several magazines cater for a popular interest developed since the early 1900s, and the founding of the German branch of the Theosophical Society reawoke interest in that country. Frau Elsbeth Ebertin began an annual prophetic almanack *Ein Blick in die Zukunft* in 1917, and a startling prediction about Hitler in her 1924 issue made her widely known and inspired interest among many Germans, which became intense in the inter-war period. The Nazi attitude toward astrology was publicly hostile but privately ambivalent, and researchers disagree about its influence on the leadership.

In England a remarkable forecast, apparently of the R 101 airship disaster, by R. H. Naylor in *The Sunday Ex-*

ABOVE The wreck of the R101, October 5, 1930, allegedly prophesied by R H Naylor in the British newspaper, the *Sunday Express*.

press, impressed the public and helped bring about the plethora of star columns which appear today in the popular press.

The United States Theosophical Society gave American interest in astrology the same impetus as the German branch had the Germans. A Theosophist, Max Heindel, popularized it through a number of books, some of which are still being reissued. In 1926 Llewellyn George founded the National Astrological Association which in 1928 became the American Federation of Astrologers. His was a scientific, non-occult approach, but it is the popular brand of character delineation and forecasting of personal destiny that appeals most widely in the US and Europe and ensures a wide sale for the many astrological books published. The demand was promoted earlier by a prosecution in 1914 of Mrs George E. Jordan, better known as Evangeline Adams (1836–1932). Her erecting of a horoscope for an individual unknown to her, who turned out to be the judge's son, so impressed the judge that he was convinced that she had "raised astrology to the dignity of an exact science." Evangeline had her own radio program in 1930, two years after the founding of the American Federation of Astrologers, which today has more than five thousand practising astrologers on its books who cater for an estimate of well over ten million clients.

How widely astrology is believed in the modern world is impossible to say. But there are few in the Western world who do not know their zodiacal sign and who, if their eyes fall on "What the Stars Foretell" in their daily paper, do not read the paragraph that concerns them, even if they smile at themselves for doing so. There is argument and evidence for and against both sides, and this is considered as objectively as possible in the next chapter.

ABOVE A hieroglyphic prognostication for the year 1865 from *Raphael's Prophetic Messenger and Almanack.*

ABOVE William Lilly, b May 1, 1602 (Taurus), English Astrologer, immortalized as Sidrophel in Samuel Butler's *Hudibras*.

CHAPTER SIX

IS ASTROLOGY FEASIBLE?

A human being is proportionately closer to the planets of the solar system than he is to the smallest particles known to science within his own body. A man 5 feet 10 inches tall (see Bibliography, Michel, Aimé) has voluntary control of particles – in groups if not individually – 1,750,000,000,000,000 times smaller than himself. If the electrons in such a human body were each to become as large as the man, he would extend to 200,000,000,000 miles. Pluto, the most distant planet, moves on an axis 4,000,000,000 miles from the Sun, or one-fiftieth the height of our giant, to whom the solar system would appear as a tiny eddy ⅕″ in diameter. Since this enormous universe which is a man can affect and be affected by the particles of which it is composed, there is nothing *a priori* impossible about the particles called humans being affected by the heavenly bodies. A human body is about a thousand times closer to Pluto in space than one of its electrons is to it in size.

"Ah," it may be replied, "but each human is a self-contained unity, quite different and separate from the inanimate masses of rock we call planets orbiting in space." To a quantum physicist, all solid matter consists of vast quantities of empty space in which orbit the particles of which matter consists. An electron is in proportion to the atom in which it has its being as a grain of salt is to the dome of St Peter's, Rome (see Bibliography, Talbot, Michael). Even this simile can lead to misconception, for electrons are pure energy, not microscopically tiny building blocks, and one of them is much more like a minute electric spark than anything solid as salt. Our Gar-

gantua, stretching his $1,750^{12}$ miles, would be relatively as full of empty space as the solar system and the realms beyond it – yet he would remain a unity, the parts of which could influence and be influenced by each other and could, furthermore, influence many other automonous systems.

What is more, he would consist of exactly the same particles as the rest of the universe. The quantum physicist finds no difficulty in surmising that the behaviour of a particle on earth can affect that of a brother particle on the outer rim of the galaxy and vice versa, and this without there being any apparent means of communication between them.

The first scientific blow against astro-science was the discovery of the precession of the equinoxes in the second century BC by the Greek astronomer Hipparchus. This is caused by a

LEFT Hipparchus, *fl* 146–127 BC, Greek astronomer, who discovered the precession of the equinoxes, one of the first scientific challenges to the claims of astrology.

very slow change in the Earth's axis of rotation which brings about a circular motion of the celestial poles among the stars, each circle taking 25,800 years to complete. This meant that 4,000 years ago the Sun at the spring equinox was in the constellation of Aries; from 300 AD it has been in that of Pisces; and from about 2000 AD it will be in that of Aquarius. The movement of the celestial poles and equator takes with it the zodiac and its signs, so that a child born under what was Taurus is now classified as a subject of Aries and given Arien characteristics. Astrological tradition therefore becomes invalid when the alignment of signs and constellations ceases, or else the qualities attributed to the signs are not connected with them at all. Astrologers reply that they use an "intellectual" zodiac and not the constellations, or make the more mystical answer that the movement is in harmony with the spiral path of the evolution of mankind.

ASTRONOMICAL CHALLENGES

The sixteenth- and seventeenth-century astronomical revelations of Copernicus, Brahe, Kepler and Galileo (page H7–8) again shook astrology, but only temporarily. The theory of gravity of Sir Isaac Newton (1642–1727) strengthened rather than weakened belief because it showed that the universe was held together by powerful yet invisible forces. It also supported a philosophy which had arisen that there was a harmony throughout creation, so that a pattern in the universe was reflected by a similar pattern among men: "as above, so below." Thus the appearance of the sky at the moment of a birth indicated a design with which the life of the infant would harmonize.

The discovery in 1781 of an eighth planet, Uranus, was a further blow to conventional astrology, as was the detection of

LEFT The theory of gravity promulgated by Sir Isaac Newton (1642–1727, born December 25 (Capricorn), strengthened belief in astrology.

LEFT Swarm of locusts in Algeria. The eleven-year cycle of sunspots at its peak allegedly produces such swarms of pests.

Neptune in 1846 and Pluto in 1930. Ever resilient, astrologers bounced back with the contention that these planets are so far away and move so slowly that they influence generations rather than individuals. The fact that they were discovered when they were, and the implications of their discovery in that they allegedly influence world movements and scientific advance, are all part of the grand scheme of things that is patterned in the heavens.

Scientific discoveries during the twentieth century have shown that the phases of the Moon have a direct effect on the reproductive system of a number of forms of life. The eleven-year cycle of sunspots appears to affect rainfall and, consequently, water levels and vegetation. It can shorten days by a fraction of a second, but enough to occasion earthquakes and volcanic eruptions. It causes proliferation of microbes and possibly epidemics, produces plagues of pests such as locusts, and is responsible for certain deficiencies in our bodies and even in our minds. Ill-health, road accidents, sudden deaths, suicides and criminal acts increase as sunspots move toward their peak of activity. Diseases of the heart and lungs are associated with solar magnetic disturbances and variations in the Sun's cycle apparently affect all aspects of life on Earth. Our world is actually within the Sun's atmosphere and where its magnetic atmosphere meets the Earth's, disturbances occur which may affect life.

For all astrology's attempts to come to terms with scientific advances, it continued to receive condemnation from different quarters. Robert Eisler, in his *The Royal Art of Astrology* wrote, somewhat exaggeratedly, of its "futile practices . . . investigated with the greatest care and impartiality by the foremost scholars of the leading Western nations for now almost three centuries . . . not one of these failed to condemn them." C. G. Jung wrote, "If astrologers had concentrated more on statistics . . . they would have found out long ago that their pronouncements rest on unstable predictions." But Jung did not dismiss astrology entirely. In 1948 he wrote to *The Indian Astrological Magazine*, "In cases of difficult psychological diagnosis I usually get a horoscope . . . I very often find that the astrological data elucidated certain points which I otherwise would have been unable to understand."

Recognizing that astrologers sometimes made startlingly true predictions, Jung attributed these not to the stars but to telepathic or clairvoyant gifts which used the horoscope as a focus to catch glimpses of the future. He also used astrology to test his theory of synchronicity. This stated that everything done at a certain moment of time had the qualities of that moment, a law that was due neither to chance nor causality. The process consisted of two factors: (1) an unconscious image emerges into consciousness either directly (as itself) or indirectly (symbolized or suggested) in the form of a dream, idea or premonition; (2) an objective situation coincides with this context. Jung partly supported his theory by analyzing 996 horoscopes of married couples, and tried to discover variations in the charts of married and non-married subjects. The frequency of the marriage conjunctions indicated only chance, but the conjunction of one partner's Sun with the other's Moon, or both partners' Moons, came first in frequency of all other aspects noted.

Jung's conception that everything done at a certain moment held the qualities of that moment combines with another modern concept, that the whole of existence is one great energy system. The atom has a nucleus, atoms make up cells which have hearts, cells make up humans with hearts at their centres; the Sun is the heart of the solar system, itself a kind of cell in the Milky Way galaxy, which is in turn a unit in a pattern of galaxies and so on; and all are made up of the same basic particles of energy, interconnected in such a way that a stone thrown into a pond on earth can cause a ripple in the farthest galaxies.

But since the stars affect men, they must influence all living creatures. Astrologers have drawn up horoscopes for pets – a logical extension to some, an absurdity to others – when is the moment of birth of a parrot?

FALSE POSITIONS AND STATISTICS

A powerful argument against astrology is that the planetary aspects drawn by practitioners are flat patterns. They establish the celestial latitude and longitude of heavenly bodies but make no allowance for distance and the velocity of light.

Even when they are relatively close, the velocity of light places them not where they appear to be but where they were at the time the light reflected from them began its journey to Earth. The apparent positions of some planets could differ from their actual places greatly enough to alter fundamentally the readings of the horoscopes. The astrologer may reply that the system he employs is a mathematically accurate two-dimensional representation of a three-dimensional reality having its own kind of perspective which is valid as that which enables a two-dimensional picture to give an illusion of three dimensions. Furthermore it is the moment of the event on earth that is significant and the combination of forces and influences that is operative at that moment.

Michel Gauquelin (born 1928), who has probably collected more astrological data than any man living quotes various experiments (see Bibliography, *Astrology and Science*), the verdict of which goes against astrology. In one, 14 practitioners, chosen haphazardly, were given birth details of three celebrities and their names and challenged to fit the dates to the names. The results could not have been worse had they answered at random. Another group, given 20 dates of birth of ten murderers and ten "dull" lives, and asked to separate one lot from the other, gave entirely chance results. Against these, Jeff Mayo (see Bibliography, *Teach Yourself Astrology*), claims that he was one of 20 astrologers who were asked to match ten birth charts with ten case histories, describing occupations. A control group of 20 who knew no astrology were asked to do the same with the same group of charts and histories. Sixteen of the 20 astrologers predicted better than chance (how much better is not stated) against nine of the controls. The fallibility of statistics of this undetailed kind is shown by the fact that if the 16 astrologers had scored six out of ten (better than chance) and four had scored five (chance), their total would have been 116; while if the nine non-astrologers had scored seven and the other eleven had scored five, their total would have been 118. It is not true to say that "one can prove anything by statistics," but the exact details must be known if the evidence is to be valid.

Statistics, astrologers would argue, are largely irrelevant because they remove the vital personal element in interpretation. Since every chart is individual, because no birth can take place at exactly the same place at the same time, statistics can deal only with certain features separately in a birth chart, whereas in fact everything is interdependent and the same features in different contexts could give different meanings. Some psychic principle is always involved.

There is a parallel in psychical research where two prin-

MICHEL GAUQUELIN: A NEW PERSPECTIVE

Since his student days at the Sorbonne, when he studied psychology and statistics with research into astrology in mind, Gauquelin has devoted many years to the application of statistics to the science. In his *Astrology and Science* he built up a sufficiently powerful case against conventional astrology as to destroy it, but only, in a sense, to create it anew. For he discovered that a statistically significant proportion of 1,084 prominent medical academicians were born when either Mars or Saturn had just risen or were at their culmination. Later he confirmed by the examination of 25,000 celebrities in Germany, Italy, Belgium, Holland and France, and many thousands since, that irrespective of national culture and background, a man's profession corresponded to the positions of certain planets at his birth.

ciples have come to be recognized, the "observer effect" and the "sheep and goats effect." The former is the recognition that, except in the exact sciences (and perhaps not even there) there can be no such event as a completely objective experiment. This is because the observer, by the very act of observing, becomes part of the experiment and exerts an influence upon it. The latter describes the tendency of believers (sheep) in the possibility of, say, extrasensory perception, to score above chance in tests confirming its existence, whereas non-believers (goats) score at or below chance. It may be that only the faith of the subject and an empathy between him and the practitioner can release in the psychologically intuitive astrologer the ability to interpret correctly all the factors in the horoscope, and that this is the only "true" astrology.

Gauquelin argues that our genetic code has stamped on it our youth, maturity and age, and predetermines particularly illnesses and accidents. The universe, including man, is subject to rhythms acting as cosmic "clocks" – can it be that the inner "clocks" of a human embryo predispose him to enter the world under certain cosmic conditions which correspond to his biological constitution, rather than that the planets influence him at birth? And that the parent's "clocks" determined conception?

Gauquelin further investigated "planetary heredity" by matching 15,000 parents and children, involving the examination of 300,000 positions of planets. He discovered a correlation between the birth skies of the parents and those of their children of which the probabilities against chance were 499,999 to one. The indications were clear for Mars, Jupiter, Saturn, the Moon and Venus. There was not enough evidence for Mercury, which is very small, nor for Uranus, Neptune and Pluto, which are very distant. The effects of hereditary characteristics were more marked in a child whose birth sky corresponded to that of his parents, but the results varied in the cases of births that were induced (as one would expect).

Writing on the birth data of his first sample of medical academicians, Gauquelin said, "Ordinary people *never* [my italics] showed this effect." What of people in limiting circumstances who could have become great doctors, given the opportunity? Or is Gauquelin to be taken literally? If he is, under what stars are "ordinary" people born?

Whatever future research may show, Gauquelin denies the thesis that planets govern professions or characters, suggesting only the biological clocks explanation. He seems not so much to have destroyed traditional astrology as to have turned it inside out. Instead of the heavens moulding the births of humans, the births have suited themselves to the heavens. Whatever the final results of research – if finality is reached before the stars have run their courses – it seems that at present an individual's belief, or not, in astrology depends on the "clocks" that determine his birthday and the planets that are where they are when he arrives.

Voyager I photograph of Saturn's moon Titan: if the planets affect us directly, sceptics claim, then why are the smaller celestial bodies ignored by astrologers in their calculations?

INDEX

BIBLIOGRAPHY

There are hundreds, even thousands, of books on astrology, from popular introductions to erudite and scholarly dissertations. The following list is not intended to be exhaustive but will serve as an introduction to the student to lead him on to still further reading.

COPE, LLOYD *Your Stars Are Numbered* Doubleday, New York, 1971

GAUQUELIN, MICHAEL *Astrology and Science* Mayflower Books, London, 1972

GOODMAN, LINDA *Sun Signs* Pan Books, London & Sydney. First Printing 1972, many reprintings since.

HEINDEL, MAX *Simplified Scientific Astrology* Melvin Powers, Wiltshire Book Company, Hollywood, California, 1989 (originally written 1928)

INNES, BRIAN *Horoscopes* Macdonald & Co., London, 1987

LEE, DAL *A Dictionary of Astrology* Sphere Books, London, 1969

MacLEOD, CHARLOTTE *Astrology for Sceptics* Turnstone Books, London, 1973

McINTOSH, CHRISTOPHER *Astrology* Macdonald Unit 75, London, 1970

The Astrologers and Their Creed Hutchinson, London, 1969

MAYO, JEFF *Teach Yourself Astrology* English Universities Press, London, 1964

The Astrologer's Astronomical Handbook Fowler, London, 1965

MICHELSON, NEIL F. *The American Ephemeris for the 20th Century 1900 to 2000, at Noon. Revised.* ACS Publications, San Diego, California, 1983.

The Koch Book of Tables ACS Publications, San Diego, California, Second Printing, 1987.

NAYLOR, P. I. H. *Astrology, an Historical Examination* Robert Maxwell, London, 1967.

RANDALL, SIDNEY *An ABC of the Old Science of Astrology* Foulsham and Co., London, 1917.

RUDHYAR, DANE *The Astrology of Personality* (2nd Edition) Servire, The Hague, 1963.

SHULMAN, SANDRA *An Encyclopedia of Astrology* Hamlyn, London, 1976.

THIERENS, A. E. *Elements of Esoteric Astrology* Rider & Co., London, 1931.

WEST, A. E. AND TOONDER, J. G. *The Case for Astrology* Macdonald, London, 1973.

WOODRUFF, BOB *Astrology for Fun* Tarnhelm Press Lakemont, Georgia, 1976.

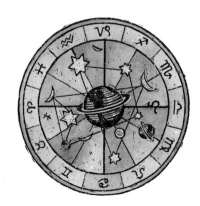